THE NAKED TRUTH

The Naked Communist – *Revisited*

James C. Bowers, Sc.D.

This book is an analysis of a specific section in the book, *The Naked Communist* by W. Cleon Skousen, published in 1958. The section evaluated is entitled, "Current Communist Goals." From his FBI background, Mr. Skousen lists what he considered to be the top **45 Goals** of the Communists, **as of 1958**. The progress and status of each of these Goals **as of 2012** is carefully documented. Prepare to be shocked!

AGENDADOCUMENTARY.com

To order additional copies
(including volume discount prices)
go to: agendadocumentary.com

The Naked Truth — The Naked Communist — *Revisited*

Copyright © 2011 by James C. Bowers

No part of this book may be reproduced or transmitted in any form or by any means electronic or mechanical, including photocopying or by any information storage without permission in writing from the copyright owner.

Second printing 2012
Third printing 2012
Fourth printing 2013
Fifth printing 2015
Sixth printing 2016
Seventh printing 2017
Eighth printing 2018
Ninth printing 2019
Tenth printing 2019
Eleventh printing 2020

Library of Congress Control Number: 2011919398

International Standard Book Number: 978-0-936163-16-1

Dedication

This book is dedicated to my wife, Carole Russell Bowers, not just for her general love and support, which is a typical reason, but for something much more direct! In 1960 she had begun reading books of a political nature. I was a student at the time, working on my doctorate in science at Washington University in St. Louis. I was also an electrical engineer working for McDonnell Aircraft Corp, involved with the Mercury spacecraft program. I had little time, knowledge or interest in things political. One day she was listening to a radio talk show and heard a Fred Schwarz, M.D. speaking about the dangers of communism – stating that we Americans needed to wake up! He mentioned that there were various "study groups" being conducted in the St. Louis area for people to attend and become more informed. That evening when I came home she said we were going to an important meeting that night. I would be embarrassed to admit what my reaction to her was after a long, hard day of work and study. Nevertheless, she persisted. That night changed my life and influenced our family's lives forever!

Acknowledgements

The author wishes to thank several others who were helpful in this endeavor. My son Curtis recently produced an award-winning Documentary ($101,000, First Place Prize) entitled: *AGENDA – Grinding America Down*. In that movie he mentions Skousen and discusses several of the Goals listed in his *Naked Communist* book. That list has always intrigued me, so I decided to follow through and investigate just how many of Skousen's Communist Goals had been accomplished. This book is a direct result of that study. To view a trailer of Curtis' movie, go to: AgendaDocumentary.com. It is fantastic! Thanks also to my daughter Kellie McGuire. She carefully edited my manuscript several times.

A special thanks to Don McAlvany (editor of the monthly **McAlvany Intelligence Advisor**). While travelling Europe, he took the time to proofread this manuscript. What a sharp eye he has, catching small errors that had been missed by everyone. With his extensive background in this area, he also offered many valuable suggestions on the material being presented.

In addition, the author wishes to thank Dr. David Noebel. As the President of **Summit Ministries** for almost 50 years, he has been a leader in training young people on world views at the Summit summer conferences. He edited this manuscript and wrote the Foreword. He recently co-authored a book with Dr. Fred Schwarz that greatly complements this work. It is entitled: ***You Can Still Trust the Communists . . . to be Communists.***

Details on the Summit youth program and ordering information for Dr. Noebel's book can be found at: summit.org.

Finally, thanks Beth. If you had been my high school English teacher, I may not have needed so many proof-readers on this project.

As mentioned in the Dedication, it was Dr. Schwarz on the radio in 1961 that led to my involvement in this battle. Years later (1980's), my elder son Clark (also very active in the fight) became a close personal friend of Dr. Schwarz. Still later, Clark introduced Dr. Schwarz to Summit Ministries (1990's), which led to Schwarz working with Dr. Noebel. Now in 2011, the Schwarz Report Press is publishing my book. It is a "small world!"

Table of Contents

FOREWORD ix
PREFACE xi
INTRODUCTION xiii
CHAPTER 1 – Goal Nos. 1, 2, 3 & 9 1
CHAPTER 2 – Goal Nos. 4, 5, & 6 25
CHAPTER 3 – Goal No. 7 35
CHAPTER 4 – Goal No. 11 39
CHAPTER 5 – Goal Nos. 12 & 13 43
CHAPTER 6 – Goal No. 14 45
CHAPTER 7 – Goal No. 15 49
CHAPTER 8 – Goal No. 16 55
CHAPTER 9 – Goal No. 17 57
CHAPTER 10 – Goal Nos. 19 & 34 63
CHAPTER 11 – Goal Nos. 20 & 21 67
CHAPTER 12 – Goal Nos. 22 & 23 71
CHAPTER 13 – Goal Nos. 24 & 25 75
CHAPTER 14 – Goal No. 26 79

CHAPTER 15 – Goal No. 27 83
CHAPTER 16 – Goal No. 28 85
CHAPTER 17 – Goal Nos. 29 & 30 91
CHAPTER 18 – Goal No. 32 97
CHAPTER 19 – Goal No. 35 117
CHAPTER 20 – Goal No. 36 121
CHAPTER 21 – Goal No. 37 125
CHAPTER 22 – Goal Nos. 38 & 39 129
CHAPTER 23 – Goal Nos. 40 & 41 133
CHAPTER 24 – Goal No. 42 137
CHAPTER 25 – Goal No. 43 141
CHAPTER 26 – Goal No. 44 143
CHAPTER 27 – Goal No. 45 145
CONCLUSIONS 147
EPILOGUE 159

Foreword

One of the strangest phenomena of our times is liberalism's affinity toward Marxism. It has now been documented that various Communist governments during the 20th Century alone have brutally murdered over 150,000,000 human beings (see R.J. Rummel, *Death By Government*). In addition to that staggering accomplishment, everywhere in the world that communism has been tried, it has been a total failure. The liberal/leftist always talks about bad weather, lack of natural resources and other excuses as the reason the Communist countries lag so far behind. How ridiculous! What about East and West Germany during the Cold War? Or even now — how do they explain North and South Korea? The Communist North is one of the poorest countries in the world and the people have zero freedom, yet the South is one of the most prosperous and free. Think about that fact! Same country, same people, same everything, except one thing: the type of government system they have!

This makes no sense, but even as I write, there are thousands of professors in our American colleges waxing eloquently on the wonders of communism/socialism/atheism; brainwashing another generation of our youth (see Thomas Sowell, *Intellectuals and Society*). In addition, there are hundreds in government positions in Washington D.C. who in spite of the above facts are pushing our country toward socialism (see Robert Chandler, *Shadow World*). The greatest form of representative government ever devised is being systematically destroyed by those who are totally blinded to reality. This book documents that this has not happened by accident. There has been a plan and the leftists have had their Goals and they have been working to accomplish these Goals for decades. Why they want to do this, I'll leave to the reader, but it seems to me like insanity!

David A. Noebel
2011

Preface

In 1958, W. Cleon Skousen authored a book entitled, *The Naked Communist*. It was quite successful at the time and has remained so for over fifty years — as it is still in print. Mr. Skousen had a remarkable career. After receiving his law degree from George Washington University, he served for many years as an FBI agent. Later, he became the Chief of Police of Salt Lake City. Also, he was the national editor of a leading police magazine, *Law and Order*. Skousen retired as a University professor in 1978. He passed away in 2006 at the age of 92.

Why background about an author of another book? The answer is very simple. This book is based on an analysis of a section of Skousen's 1958 book where he listed what he perceived then as the, "Current Communist Goals." With his background as an FBI agent, he was very familiar with the plans and goals of the Communists. In his book he listed forty-five of those Goals. With his access and insight into the Communists' plans, the Goals he listed have, unfortunately, largely come to pass — even after the USSR collapsed and many in America assumed, "the cold war was over."

As will be seen, what has happened in these fifty plus years has been accomplished very subtly and very quietly. In the early years, the goals pushed forward by American Marxists and other leftwing sympathizers were controlled and financed, in large part, by the Soviet Union. However, the progressives were so entrenched in the power-centers of America that even when the

USSR crumbled because of President Reagan's peace through strength policies, the subversive work continued full-speed ahead. Shockingly, we have now come to the place in America where the final implementation of these Goals is being carried out, not by outside individuals or groups, but by people in our own country. As is carefully documented within these pages, it will be clearly seen that many in the Obama Administration are working feverishly to complete this task of turning America into a Socialist-style "global" nation. Unfortunately, the "main-stream" media has covered up all of this, keeping the public almost completely in the dark.

The most unexpected aspect of Skousen's analysis is that many of the Goals listed are apparently based on his understanding that the pure Marxist approach would not work in America and that the real threat would come from the radicals within our midst following the "Gramsci" model. Many of even the most informed people in 1958 probably had never even heard of Gramsci. It is a very simple strategy and will later be discussed and explained. The native Italian Antonio Gramsci's theory of "cultural hegemony" outlined a unique method for a Marxist takeover of an advanced Capitalistic country. Regrettably, it has been remarkably effective.

A quick, bird's eye view of the Communists' success in the last fifty years can be seen by simply noting how the Communists were viewed in 1958, compared to now. In 1958 one would be sued if they called anyone a Communist, because at that time communism was the system of government that most people identified with economic disaster, total loss of freedom, enslavement, starvation and the brutal murder of literally tens of millions of people in countries around the world. They were considered evil, hostile enemies who were trying to takeover the entire planet. They were America's supreme enemy. Flash forward to 2009, when an openly admitted Communist is appointed to a high advisory position by Barrack Obama, the President of the United States. That's a significant change in a relatively short period of time.

Introduction

The Gramsci theory mentioned in the Preface is based upon Antonio Gramsci's writings in the 1920's. It is not complicated. His approach about how communism could replace capitalism was different from the pure Marxian model. He analyzed why the Marxist approach would never be successful in a religious-based, Western style country. Gramsci theorized that in a country like America, it would first be necessary to **undermine the culture and morality**, before the people would accept the slide into socialism. He discarded a Marxist concept that the overthrow would come from a "revolt of the workers." Gramsci insisted that it would only succeed by having the intellectuals and elites working to change the country's culture from within. The final destruction of our American way of life would not be completed by external Communists, but rather by dedicated American progressives.

The forty-five "Current Communist Goals" listed in Skousen's 1958 book are listed and the status of each will be analyzed in the Chapters to follow. In many cases entire books have been written (in some cases many books) to document a specific point. These books were not written to address Skousen's predictions, but rather to prove a dangerous trend in a specific area. With forty-five Goals to be analyzed, obviously it is not planned on having a book length Chapter on each topic. Rather, a summary or overview is given that will suffice to prove the point to an unbiased reader. However, for those wishing more detail and support, References are listed at the end of each Chapter, where readers will find, beyond a shadow of a doubt, that the summary conclusions made herein are fair and accurate.

Probably the most important aspect of reviewing these Goals is remembering that they were written in 1958. People are suspicious of the "Monday morning quarterbacks" who can always explain, after the fact, why certain things happen. As with the Bible, one of the most powerful things proving its validity is the fact that the prophecies made centuries before, ultimately all came to pass exactly as predicted. So, as you are reading these Goals, keep reminding yourself that this was all in writing over fifty years ago. That most of the Goals have already been accomplished, exactly as Skousen stated, would seem to be proof that the leftists did have a plan, they did have an agenda and they have been diligently working to carry it out. Could all of these Goals be accomplished by accident? Is it ignorance or treason?

The difficulty in discussing some of these Goals is that many younger Americans have never known when some of these were not the norm in America. For example, how many readers know that for decades it was illegal to import **anything** into America that was produced in Communist China? Hard to imagine today, when almost everything we buy today is, "Made in China." Also, does anyone remember that for decades, people working for the government had to take a "loyalty oath?" Furthermore, the average American today is probably not aware of the historical fact that for several hundred years of our country's history, almost all schools and colleges in America were founded by Christians, the Bible was a standard textbook, the Ten Commandments were posted in the schools and prayer opened each school day. One simple, but stark, example of this complete turnaround is Harvard University. It is now a very liberal, secular college – actually hostile to Christianity, yet it was founded as a Christian college to train pastors. Its early motto was *Veritas Christo et Ecclesiae*, "Truth for Christ and the Church." Only in the past fifty years have all of these Biblical foundations and traditions gradually been ruled unconstitutional, **even though they were all accepted and practiced by the people who wrote the Constitution.** Strange, indeed!

As will be seen, some of these Goals are not as significant as others and a few are no longer applicable, since the breakup of the Soviet Union and the unification of Germany. In addition, many of these Goals might seem to the uninformed person to be totally unrelated to any plan to pave the way for a Communist victory. Keep two things in mind: First, the Marxists have been using the "Gramsci Model" in America, which requires that our culture be broken down as a first step. Secondly, it was the Communists who came up with these Goals — so whether they make sense to us or not is immaterial. Overall, Skousen's predictions are incredibly accurate. It is important to remember that his predictions were not based on a crystal ball, but upon his vast knowledge of communism, through his years at the FBI and other law enforcement positions. Therefore, they are not really predictions in that sense; rather Skousen was in a position to know exactly what their plans were. He just summarized them in print – giving us a "heads up." We ignore this evil progress at our own peril. We must understand that all of these trends and events in America for the past fifty years have not happened by accident. They were laid out years ago as a part of the Communist strategy to take over the world – just as their Marxist founders openly proclaimed they would.

Current Communist Goals (1958)

1. U.S. acceptance of co-existence as the only alternative to atomic war.
2. U.S. willingness to capitulate in preference to engaging in atomic war.
3. Develop the illusion that total disarmament by the United States would be a demonstration of moral strength.
4. Permit free trade between all nations regardless of Communist affiliation and regardless of whether or not items could be used for war.
5. Extension of long-term loans to Russia and Soviet satellites.
6. Provide American aid to all nations regardless of Communist domination.
7. Grant recognition of Red China. Admission of Red China to the UN.

8. Set up East and West Germany as separate states in spite of Khrushchev's promise in 1955 to settle the Germany question by free elections under supervision of the UN.
9. Prolong the Conferences to ban atomic tests, because the U.S. has agreed to suspend tests as long as negotiations are in progress.
10. Allow all Soviet satellites individual representation in the UN.
11. Promote the UN as the only hope for mankind. If its charter is rewritten, demand that it be set up as one-world government with its own independent armed forces.
    (Some Communist leaders believe the world can be taken over as easily by the UN as by Moscow. Sometimes these two centers compete with each other.)
12. Resist any attempt to outlaw the Communist Party.
13. Do away with all loyalty oaths.
14. Continue giving Russia access to the U.S. Patent Office.
15. Capture one or both of the political parties in the U.S.
16. Use technical decisions of the courts to weaken basic American institutions by claiming their activities violate civil rights.
17. Get control of the schools. Use them as transmission belts for socialism and current Communist propaganda. Soften the curriculum. Get control of teachers' associations. Put the party line in text-books.
18. Gain control of all student newspapers.
19. Use student riots to foment public protests against programs or organizations which are under Communist attack.
20. Infiltrate the press. Get control of book-review assignments, editorial writing, policy-making positions.
21. Gain control of key positions in radio, TV, and motion pictures.
22. Continue discrediting American culture by degrading all forms of artistic expression. An American Communist cell was told to "eliminate all good sculpture from parks and buildings; substitute shapeless, awkward, and meaningless forms."
23. Control art critics and directors of art museums. "Our plan is to promote ugliness, repulsive, meaning-less art."

24. Eliminate all laws governing obscenity by calling them "censorship" and a violation of free speech and free press.
25. Break down cultural standards of morality by promoting pornography and obscenity in books, magazines, motion pictures, radio, and TV.
26. Present homo-sexuality, degeneracy, and promiscuity as "normal, natural, healthy."
27. Infiltrate the churches and replace revealed religion with "social religion." Discredit the Bible and emphasize the need for intellectual maturity which does not need a "religious crutch."
28. Eliminate prayer or any phase of religious expression in the schools on the ground that it violates the principle of "separation of church and state."
29. Discredit the American Constitution by calling it inadequate, old-fashioned, out of step with modern needs, a hindrance to co-operation between nations on a worldwide basis.
30. Discredit the American founding fathers. Present them as selfish aristocrats who had no concern for the "common man."
31. Belittle all forms of American culture and discourage the teaching of American history on the ground that it was only a minor part of "the big picture." Give more emphasis to Russian history since the Communists took over.
32. Support any Socialist movement to give centralized control over any part of the culture — education, social agencies, welfare programs, mental health clinics, etc.
33. Eliminate all laws or procedures which interfere with the operation of the Communist apparatus.
34. Eliminate the House Committee on Un-American Activities.
35. Discredit and eventually dismantle the FBI.
36. Infiltrate and gain control of more unions.
37. Infiltrate and gain control of big business.
38. Transfer some of the powers of arrest from the police to social agencies. Treat all behavioral problems as psychiatric disorders which no one but psychiatrists can understand or treat.

39. Dominate the psychiatric profession and use mental health laws as a means of gaining coercive control over those who oppose Communist goals.
40. Discredit the family as an institution. Encourage promiscuity and easy divorce.
41. Emphasize the need to raise children away from the negative influence of parents. Attribute prejudices, mental blocks, and retarding of children to suppressive influence of parents.
42. Create the impression that violence and insurrection are legitimate aspects of the American tradition; that students and special-interest groups should rise up and use "united force" to solve economic, political or social problems.
43. Overthrow all colonial governments before native populations are ready for self-government.
44. Internationalize the Panama Canal.
45. Repeal the Connally Reservation so the United States cannot prevent the World Court from seizing jurisdiction over domestic problems. Give the World Court jurisdiction over nations and individuals alike.

The intension of this book is to summarize the events which confirm that a particular Goal has been accomplished or is well on the way. As mentioned, reference materials will be given in each area, for those interested in further study. Some of these reference books are classics, but may be out of print. However, used copies can almost always be found on Amazon.com. It is important to mention that several of the shortest Chapters of this book are actually the most significant. The reason those vital issues are not expanded upon herein is that they are the most widely known and heavily documented areas, with no need to duplicate here. Rather, more time is spent exposing in more detail the lesser known Goals.

Reference: *The Naked Communist*, W. Cleon Skousen, 1958, Ensign Publ. Co.

CHAPTER ONE

Goal No. 1: U.S. acceptance of coexistence as the only alternative to atomic war.
Goal No. 2: U.S. willingness to capitulate in preference to engaging in atomic war.
Goal No. 3: Develop the illusion that total disarmament by the United States would be a demonstration of moral strength.
Goal No. 9: Prolong the Conferences to ban atomic tests, because the U.S. has agreed to suspend tests as long as negotiations are in progress.

These four Goals listed above have been intertwined during the last fifty years. While implementing these four Goals, almost 40 countries were swept under Communist domination. The shocking and sad part of this Chapter is that it documents the fact that decisions made in America, by the traitors or dupes in our midst, led to far more disasters than any overt actions by hostile nations during this time frame. "Dupes" was a term commonly used by the FBI in the 50's and 60's. It is not referring to unintelligent people, but rather normal people from all walks of life who are deceived into helping the Communist cause without realizing it. Stalin called them "useful idiots."

Although the concept of, "Better Red Than Dead" was unthinkable in 1958, by the late 1960's it became a popular and widely accepted catchphrase. The era of "peaceful coexistence" was promoted by the Soviets from World War II until the early 1970's, when the Communist buzzword of "détente" was slowly exchanged and accepted by Washington and most of the American media. The goal of both slogans was to keep America on the sidelines of the world conflicts, terrified by the thought of nuclear war – as the U.S.S.R. gobbled up country after country. We were told daily by the politicians and the media that we had no choice. It was negotiations, standing by or nuclear war. School children were programmed to fear a nuclear attack. Endless, dangerous and unenforceable treaties were negotiated and signed by the U.S.S.R. and the U.S.A. during this time. As Skousen predicted, all of these treaties were used against us. Just how effectively is summarized by the following article:

> The Soviets have always been explicit about their intentions — so was Hitler in *Mein Kamp*f.
>
> Objective truth has no place in Communist morality, by their own statements. Any statement that will advance the cause of world communism is regarded as truthful, acceptable, and perfectly normal. As far back as 1919, Zinoviev put it well in a statement that applies to the Viet Cong and the Sandinistas as much as to the revolutionary Bolsheviks: We are willing to sign an unfavorable peace. It would only mean we should put no trust whatever in the piece of paper we should sign. We should use the breathing space so obtained in order to gather our strength. This immoral dogma — moral only in Marxist ideology — was emphasized by Joseph Stalin: Words must have no relations to actions — otherwise what kind of diplomacy is it? Words are one thing, actions another. Good words are a mask for concealment of our deeds. Sincere diplomacy is no more possible than dry water or wooden iron. In 1955 the staff of the U.S. Senate Committee on the Judiciary examined the Soviet historical record and, not unexpectedly in the light of the foregoing statements, came to the following conclusion:
>
> The staff studied **nearly a thousand treaties** and agreements ...

both bilateral and multilateral, which the Soviets have entered into not only with the United States, but with countries all over the world. The staff found that in the 38 short years since the Soviet Union came into existence, its government had broken its word to virtually every country to which it ever gave a signed promise. It signed treaties of nonaggression with neighboring states and then absorbed those states. It signed promises to refrain from revolutionary activity inside the countries with which it sought "friendship" and then cynically broke those promises. It was violating the first agreement it ever signed with the United States at the very moment the Soviet envoy, Litvinov, was putting his signature to that agreement, and it is still violating the same agreement in 1955. It broke the promises it made to the Western nations during previous meetings "at the summits" in Teheran and Yalta. It broke lend-lease agreements offered to it by the United States in order to keep Stalin from surrendering to the Nazis. It violated the charter of the United Nations. It keeps no international promises at all unless doing so is clearly advantageous to the Soviet Union. [We] seriously doubt whether during the whole history of civilization any nation has ever made as perfidious a record as this in so short a time. More recently in the 1970s and 1980s the Soviets have broken the SALT treaties and used the era of detente to develop an awe-inspiring weapons arsenal. Consequently, the history of Soviet foreign relations from 1917 to the present suggests, for those who can interpret history, two conclusions: 1. The Soviets will not keep their word in any foreign agreement. 2. Their intent is self-admittedly aggressive, with world conquest as the ultimate goal.[1]

Even after this abysmal track record, the negotiations continue to this day. In early 2011, Obama called it a great triumph of his administration that he signed the START Treaty with Russia. Many informed observers warned that this was just more of the same — tying our hands, while Russia continued on with their advances behind the scenes. Of course, Communist China is now manipulating us in military and trade deals as well. When does it stop? As will be discussed later, President Reagan proved we did have options other than surrender or die. Actually, we had very obvious options all along – we just did not use them. Instead, we allowed conferences, treaties, negotiations, disarmament traps, coalition governments, military force, appeasement and intimidation to create the disasters summarized in Charts A & B to follow. Chart A details the countries which fell to communism from World War II until 1980. It can be noted that while America was celebrating its victory after WWII (1944-45), the Reds were taking maximum advantage in those very early years. It will be shown in the summaries to follow that most of these countries were "pushed" into the Communist orbit, **not by Soviet might**, but by strategic *political* decisions made by the U.S. State Department and our Presidents. Many of the countries that were betrayed early on were done so at the Tehran, Yalta and Potsdam Conferences in 1944 — 1945. (The reference books listed at the end of this Chapter will document the details about how each of these countries was "sold out" by America, to our everlasting shame.) A vast majority of Americans would have opposed these back-door deals, but they never knew the true facts. Who made those decisions and why were they never held accountable? An early example of the naiveté (or worse) occurred when President Roosevelt met at the Yalta Conference with Prime Minister Churchill of Great Britain and Stalin, the dictator of the Soviet Union. They were trying to establish an agenda for governing post-war Germany and dealing with the other war-torn European countries. Churchill's Soviet policy differed vastly from that of Roosevelt, with Churchill believing Stalin to be a "devil-like" tyrant leading a vile system (which of course was true). Roosevelt had a different evaluation of the brutal Communist dictator Stalin. He said to Churchill:

> I just have a hunch that Stalin is not that kind of man. Harry [Hopkins] says he's not and that he [Stalin] doesn't want anything except security for his own country, and I think that if I give him everything I possibly can and ask nothing from him in return, *noblesse oblige*, he won't try to annex anything and will work with me for a world of democracy and peace.[2]

With this preposterous thinking by our President, is it any

wonder that such disastrous and tragic consequences followed? On second thought, if several of your top advisors and "some of your best friends" are Communists, what would one expect? As a case in point, note that Roosevelt was justifying his opinion by what he had heard from a top advisor, Harry Hopkins. Unfortunately, former Russian KGB agent Oleg Gordievsky has identified Hopkins as a Soviet agent "of major significance" in his book, *KGB: The Inside Story*. As a result of that treasonous advice and distorted thinking by FDR, over twelve of the countries listed in Chart A were negotiated into the Red Orbit without a shot being fired and with no concern for the millions of innocent people entrapped. Just one example of how these countries were "sold out" is fully documented in the book; *I Saw Poland Betrayed*, by Arthur Bliss Lane. An important aspect of this book is that Lane was the U.S. Ambassador to Poland from 1944 to 1947. He saw firsthand how our government betrayed Poland and shoved it into the Communist orbit. Even though he had been appointed by a Democrat President, his conscience forced him to forsake his career in order to document the truth of the tragedy.

The deceit continued, but as usual the truth didn't come out until much later. For example, it wasn't until 1960 when the evidence finally surfaced that explained the reason for America's strange inaction when the people of Hungary were desperately trying to free themselves during the "Hungarian Revolt" of 1956. The quote from the telegram below, which came out four years too late, explains everything. It was recorded in the Congressional Record of August 31, 1960 (Pg. 17407):

> You will recall the revolution broke out on October 23, 1956 and that by October 28, the Hungarian patriots had rid their country of the Russian oppressors. A revolutionary regime took over and there was political hiatus for 5 days. Then the State Department of the United States, allegedly concerned about the delicate feeling of the Communist dictator Tito sent him the following cabled assurance of our national intentions in the late afternoon of Friday, November 2, 1956. **"The government of the United states does not look with favor upon governments unfriendly to the Soviet**

Union on the borders of the Soviet Union." It was no accident or misjudgment of consequences which led the imperial Russian Army to reinvade Hungary at 4 a.m. on the morning of November 4, 1956. It took less than 48 hours for him (Tito) to relay this message of treason to his superiors in the Kremlin. All the world knows the terrible consequences of that go ahead signal.

It was always assumed that America just stood by while this tragedy unfolded. That was bad enough. Many said that all we would have had to do was to quickly offer diplomatic recognition to the new, free government of Hungary and the Soviets would not have dared to move back in. As was later exposed by the telegram quoted above, the fact is those traitors working within our midst never leave anything to chance. Who wrote that telegram? Who authorized it? No one was ever asked, so a country of millions of people remained in slavery for many more years. The ironic part of all of this is that for years the *Voice of America* broadcasts were regularly encouraging the entrapped people of Eastern Europe to overthrow their Soviet captors and we would be there to help them. When they did, we betrayed them completely!

In the late 1950's, the agitation in Cuba was very reminiscent of how the media dealt with the agitation in China. Just as Mao had been described as a wonderful "agrarian reformer," Fidel Castro was widely called the "Robin Hood" of Cuba, out for social justice against the evil President of Cuba, the antiCommunist, pro-America Fulgencio Batista. The U.S. media went out of their way to build up Castro. Herbert Matthews of the New York Times did a series of front page reports from Cuba, praising Castro. Ed Sullivan on his popular TV show called him someone in the "great American tradition of George Washington." Informed sources knew of Castro's Communist ties. Both of our Ambassadors to Cuba warned the U.S. State Department under President Eisenhower that aiding Castro would be a great victory for international communism and a strategic defeat for the U.S.A. At a critical time, our Congress voted for a full embargo on Batista, just as they had done to the anti-Communist Chang Kai-Shek in

China. At that time the media was propagandizing how wonderful Castro would be for Cuba, while they were exposing alleged corruption in the Batista government. Undoubtedly some of that was true, but isn't it interesting (and very sad for the people) how the leftist solution is always many times worse? Cuba was a vibrant country before, but now for over 50 years the people have had little freedom and the country is in shambles.

The trend continued throughout the 1960's & 70's, where we read a steady stream of "strange" headlines that should have caused a reasonably informed person to ask the question, "Whose side are we on?"

A *Saturday Evening Post* editorial on October 14, 1961 had just such a headline:

ARE WE HELPING DELIVER THE CONGO TO THE COMMUNISTS?

The article went on to document how the U.S. seemed to be doing everything in our power to undermine the Pro-American, anti-Communist government of the Congo, in the heart of Africa. As usual our State Department succeeded in their sickening goal. First the Communist Dictator Lumumba came to power and then the Communist General Mobutu. At first they used the old trick of changing the name of their country to Zaire. Realizing that even the most informed Americans usually don't follow the details, this name-change strategy often gets the evil-doers a free pass. People simple don't remember, "Who's on first?"

The stream of confusing headlines continued. On April 20, 1964, the front page headline of the *St. Louis Globe Democrat* read:

ANTI-REDS SEIZE POWER IN LOAS

Obviously, one would expect the sub-headline below to read that America rejoiced at this answer to prayer. Remember, we were fighting a war against the Communists of North Vietnam at the time. Having a new, anti-Communist ally that bordered

North Vietnam would have been of great strategic significance. Unfortunately, the U.S. leadership was not happy with this turn of events. Therefore, the sub-headline incredibly read:

U.S. Seeks to Restore Neutralist Regime

This so-called "neutralist" regime was a Communist-dominated coalition government, as everyone acknowledged. So the logical question is why the U.S. would want a pro-Communist government in Laos. Our soldiers were fighting and dying by the thousands, supposedly to keep South Vietnam from being taken over by the Communists. Why would our government be moving to keep the Reds in power in a neighboring country? Who was making these decisions and why weren't they ever held accountable? Was this an aberration? Unfortunately not!

Six years later the same scenario unfolded with a different

1944 Lithuania	1948 Czechoslovakia
1944 Latvia	1949 China
1944 Estonia	1950 N. Korea invades S. Korea
1944 Poland	1954 North Vietnam
1944 Bulgaria	1959 Cuba
1944 Rumania	1975 South Vietnam
1944 Eastern Finland	1975 Laos
1944 Hungary	1976 Angola
1945 Yugoslavia	1976 Mozambique
1945 Albania	1978 Ethiopia
1945 East Germany	1978 South Yemen
1945 Eastern Austria	1979 Cambodia
1945 North Korea	1979 Grenada
1945 Sakhalin Island	1979 Nicaragua
1945 Kurile Island	

Countries Falling to Communism – 1944 to 1980
CHART A

country. Cambodia also borders Vietnam. A pro-Communist government was in control. The headlines from the *Tampa Tribune* of March 19, 1970 read:

CAMBODIAN PRINCE IS OUSTED AS RULER

SIDE NOTE: It is interesting to see that Communist dictators are almost always referred to in the U.S. media as Prince, Chairman, President, etc. However, if a country is under an anti-Communist leader, he is often referred to as right wing, strongman, dictator, henchman, etc. If you want to test the veracity of this statement, be my guest. Google: "Castro, Britannica." Then note the summary given. The evil Communist Dictator Castro is referred to in Britannica only as a "Political Leader" and as the "Premier" of Cuba. Do the same Google search with the duly elected, anti-Communist President Batista of Cuba, and see the results given by the Encyclopedia Britannica that is supposedly accepted as the "standard." It refers to President Batista only as, "Dictator."

It turns out that the Cambodian "Prince" was actually in Moscow with his Russian buddies when the coup took place. With a Republican in the White House in 1970, surely Nixon would be very encouraged with this news, while the war in neighboring Vietnam was still raging. Unfortunately, that was not the case, as is seen by the sub-headline:

Cambodia Coup Threatens to upset Nixon's Policy

Under the sub-headline, the UPI story read: "The rise of an anti-Communist government in Cambodia will bring joy to Saigon, but apprehension to Washington." (Saigon was the Capital city of South Vietnam, where our soldiers were fighting). The question is, at the time we were fighting a war with the Communists in Vietnam, what kind of "policies" were in place in Washington that would be "threatened" by the overthrow of a Communist government anywhere, much less on the borders of Vietnam? As usual, most Americans were taking care of their families, going to work, living their lives and were oblivious to all of this, even though it was in the headlines. They assumed that their own government had their best interest at heart. Perhaps many in the government do, but as we have seen, there is a contingent of leftists within our midst that is pushing vigorously to accomplish their Goals. A serious question is why none of the "good guys" have ever called the "bad guys" to account for their never ending series of wrong decisions? The final consequences of this Red rule in Cambodia led to the takeover by an even more radical group. The Khmer Rouge group would later sweep through Cambodia, killing about one-third of the entire population of seven million! A bloodshed so vast that even the liberal New York Times was shocked (they usually overlook Communist atrocities, as in their minds, the ends justify the means, and they apparently love the idea of a Socialist world.) A bestselling book and a major motion picture entitled, *The Killing Fields* documented this tragedy. Still, no one in America whose decisions led to this was ever exposed. Ignorance or treason?

Another major disaster in the decade of the 1970's occurred in the African country of Rhodesia. The Communists had a much easier rallying cry to take over this country than most of their usual instigations. Rhodesia had a white government in a country with a vast black majority. Using this as the cover, the drumbeats began. Naturally no country is perfect, and certainly a better balance of control would be desirable. But the Communists are never really interested in the people, only the excuse. The headlines of the *Tampa Tribune* of September 19, 1976 read:

RHODESIA GIVEN U.S. ULTIMATUM

The sub-headline read:

Told Blacks Must Rule

Many people reading this might think that is only fair – but think about it. The United States is telling another sovereign country what they are supposed to do. OK, but why are we never telling any Communist governments that they must step down? Percentagewise, there are fewer Communist Party members in most Communist countries than there are whites in Rhodesia. Is this consistent? Another important factor is that in country after country, when we help the Communist gain control by objecting to something about the anti-Communist government already in power, the final result is always exponentially worse than the situation we were supposedly trying to help! Rhodesia is a prime example. For most of the twentieth century, Rhodesia was considered the "breadbasket" of Africa. Let us fast forward thirty years to see how wonderfully the black people have benefitted by having the Communists take over their country:

> The nation once fed itself and helped feed its neighbors, but now a third of its population depends on international food handouts. Unemployment stands at 80% the same percentage that survives on less than $1 a day. Inflation is the highest in the world at more than 100,000 per cent and people suffer crippling shortages of food, water, electricity, fuel and medicine.[3]

That article is from 2008. Isn't communism wonderful? In order to hide its great "progress," the country changed its name from Rhodesia to Zimbabwe. Knowing that most people don't ever follow events to check on results, this was a logical move. Have the people in the U.S. government who made the decision to force the existing Rhodesian government to step aside ever been called to account? Have they ever acknowledged the results of their disastrous decisions? Have they even apologized to the suffering people who are paying for their "mistakes?" Note Figure 1 below to see socialism in action in a practical way that the average American can understand. **Fifty Trillion Dollars for a loaf of bread!** How does that read to any of you on a fixed income? Is this the kind of "change" campaigner Obama said, "we can believe in?"

THE NAKED TRUTH

Figure 1

During the middle of the crises, Prime Minister Smith of Rhodesia tried to warn the American people as to what the U.S. government was doing, but to no avail. He is quoted in a UPI dispatch (October 8, 1978) while trying to gain support in the U.S. against the "Marxist terrorists" trying to topple his government. "It seems the leaders of the free world are siding with the Marxist terrorists," Smith told a news conference in Virginia. Sadly the free world leaders prevailed and Rhodesia was destroyed, along with its people, both black and white.

The endless stream of contradictory headlines continued. Contradictory in the sense that communism was the only external threat to America during these years. We were spending billions of dollars, incurring a huge national debt to arm ourselves against this evil force on the one hand while moving heaven and earth to help it on the other. Americans were well aware of the billions of defense dollars spent to protect us and supported it, but few realized the other side of the deceptive coin.

On September 3, 1978, a *Tampa Tribune* article was titled:

Somoza Blaming U.S. and Cuba For Siege

In 1978 the battle lines moved into our hemisphere again. The Communists were intent on overthrowing Nicaragua. As the Communist guerrillas were fighting underground, President Somoza of Nicaragua blamed Havana and Washington for its troubles. He called out Cuba for supporting the revolt and the United States for its "blindness to the Communist threat."[4] Of course Cuba was being supplied by the Soviet Union. As to the U.S. "blindness," it is apparent that President Somoza had not been following recent U.S. history. If so, he would have noted that the U. S. is almost always on the side of the Red advances. Later, he was able to belatedly "get the picture" when our Secretary of State Cyrus Vance blatantly declared, "There has been a breakdown of trust between the government and the people of Nicaragua." Of course, Vance's solution was for the anti-Communist President Somoza to step down "as an initial move toward national reconciliation." Vance went on to add, "We must then seek a political solution which will take into account the interest of all significant groups in Nicaragua. Such a solution must begin with the replacement of the present government."[5] (Translation: The anti-Communist government must step down, so a Communist dominated government can be installed.) The Communists did take over and Somoza had to flee to Mexico where he was murdered, because he had learned the details of U.S. involvement and had to be silenced. A few years later, President Reagan was instrumental in restoring Nicaragua to freedom. Unfortunately, after he left office, the Reds regained control.

The strangest continuing story of all involves Cuba. As has already been documented, it was the American media and our policies that helped Castro gain power in Cuba. Our government's official policy (through all Democrat and Republican administrations) since 1960 is that Cuba is a dangerous enemy to its own people and to the United States. Not too many years ago, the Soviet Union was installing offensive missiles in Cuba, aimed at us. There is a strict travel and trade ban on Cuba. For many years Cuba was openly supplying aid, troops and arms to help overthrow any and all Central and South American countries who were vulnerable. We were spending considerable funds to monitor and control the Cuban threat. The bottom line is that Cuba represented the well known enemy in our hemisphere.

With those facts summarized, it is very enlightening (disgusting) to review more of the headlines over the past forty years regarding our actual policy on Cuba, behind the rhetoric. Notice carefully who the U. S. was actually targeting in these headlines. After highlighting several, some summary remarks will be offered.

The headlines from the *St. Louis Post Dispatch* of March 30, 1964 read:

U.S. PLANS STEPS TO HALT RAIDS BY CUBAN EXILES IN MOVE TO EASE TENSION

The *Colorado Springs Gazette* of July 3, 1972:

Anti-Castro Plot Smashed by U.S.

The *Tampa Tribune* of August 16, 1977:

U.S. Officials Foil Exile Raid On Cuba

The *Tampa Tribune* of January 24, 1992:

U.S. Pledges To Help Block Raids On Cuba

Under this heading the article went on to read that, "the Bush Administration vowed on Thursday to alert Cuban authorities in order to stop future raids. We will cooperate with Cuba and will advise Cuba of acts or events that take place in the U.S. that may result in actions against Cuba."

Think about these four (of many) headlines that openly state that while our government leaders in their campaign speeches are urging the Cuban people to overthrow their Communist tyrant, we are using all of our national resources to make sure they never do. What hypocrisy! What deceit! What treason?

Two Exceptions

The two exceptions in Chart A are North Korea and North Vietnam. They are exceptions in the sense that those two countries were involved in a military war involving U. S. soldiers, instead of by diplomatic treachery.

Books have documented the fact that because of political decisions, our military was not allowed to win in Korea, but rather we accepted a stalemate between North Korea and South Korea, after the loss of over 33,000 American soldiers who died trying to free all of Korea. Under the false illusion promoted, no doubt, by the many Communist agents within our government, America agreed in 1945 to let Korea be divided into two parts – forming North Korea and South Korea. One excuse for this was that if we let the Soviets have control of one half of Korea after WWII, they would "help" us in our fight against Japan, which was the country occupying Korea at that time. Of course, at that late date, the United States did not need any help defeating Japan, since the Atomic Bomb was on the way. So this diplomatic decision simply turned over half of Korea to the Communists and doomed those citizens in North Korea to pay the price — which they are still paying today.

As usual, after a period of time, the insatiable appetite of communism came into play. Not ever satisfied with just half a loaf, the Communist Army of North Korea invaded South Korea on June 25, 1950. When this happened it was a shock to the American people. With WWII only recently ended, Americans questioned, "How could this be?" "Wasn't Russia our ally fighting Germany?" "Didn't we save them?" "What's going on?" For a change the American people were awakened and upset. It was obvious to those in Washington that this overt action by the Communists could not be ignored, so President Truman was forced to move into action. Instead of America moving quickly and decisively, we went to the United Nations for a vote on protecting and defending South Korea. The U.N. did move, but with most of the troops supplied by America. After fighting a no-win war for over three years an armistice was signed. The countries remained as before, half slave and half free. While the media tried to put a happy face on this conclusion, people were upset. This frustration was intensified when President Truman fired General MacArthur during the war. MacArthur's mistake was in trying to win the war, when the progressives had other goals. Truman apparently never understood the forces at work, so he was easily agitated by his leftist advisors into firing MacArthur for insubordination.

Because of the public outcry, after the armistice was signed a congressional committee investigated the situation. The testimony of several of the generals tells the shameful tale. General Stratemeyer testified that, "You get in war to win it, you do not get into war to stand still and lose it and we were required to lose it, we were not permitted to win!" General Mark Clark stated that, "I was not allowed to bomb the numerous bridges across the Yalu River, over which the enemy constantly poured its trucks, munitions and its killers." General Douglas MacArthur testified: "Such a limitation upon the utilization of available military force to repel an enemy attack has no precedent in our own history, or as far as I know, in the history of the world."[6]

Vietnam was our next "no-win" war. Sad to report, but in Vietnam the results were far worse than Korea. First, we did nothing as the Reds moved into Vietnam. Then we sat by as the French tried to pacify them (peace at any price) and agreed to partition the country into a Communist North Vietnam and a free South Vietnam. Of course the people of North Vietnam had no say in the matter. Then after waiting for the appropriate time, the Communists moved in to takeover the rest of Vietnam. They were more subtle this time. In Korea they had moved in with a massive Army invasion. This time they just moved here and there, slowly but surely with guerilla warfare. President Kennedy was concerned by this turn of events. He felt that if South Vietnam fell to the Reds, the "dominos" in that region would all follow, right through Laos, Cambodia and Thailand.

As with the Korean War, America fought the Vietnam War with a "no-win" policy. The war lasted well over ten years. **No conflict has been more misrepresented by the media**. The fact is the war could have literally been won overnight! It is not the purpose of this book to analyze these wars in detail. But, it does fit into the scope of this book to point out how our policies were being controlled by people who did not have our best interests at heart. This explains why the "Goals" being discussed have been so quickly and methodically accomplished. As for an "overnight" victory, one need look no further than the speech given by Gen. John McConnell, who was the Air Force Chief of Staff at the time. In Detroit on December 6, 1965 he said categorically, "It is true that we could achieve this objective (*total victory*), virtually overnight. We certainly have the military capability to do so. But President Johnson has emphasized that it is our national policy to keep the conflict at the lowest possible level of intensity, for humanitarian as well as political reasons." Question: How is it humane to drag on a war for over ten years and to have thousands die in a war that could have been won overnight? Just who was advising President Johnson and what were their goals?

Some may have falsely assumed that Gen. McConnell was referring to dropping Atomic bombs and killing hundreds of thousands of people. This was not his strategy. Other military men spoke out about how simple it would be to end the war quickly, with very little loss of life on both sides. It was pointed out that the destruction of the dams above the capital city of Hanoi would put that city under 10 feet of water.[7] Quite wet, but not life-threatening. It is estimated that Hanoi internally supplied about 20% of the war materials. Other military strategists pointed out the obvious, that a barge or any large ship could be sunk in Haiphong harbor which would then block the dredges from keeping the shipping channel open (Haiphong is not a "natural" harbor and requires constant dredging to keep the shipping channel open). This would end the other 80% of the war materials – the supplies that were being shipped in from other countries. Consider what you have just read. Two conventional bombs (one on the dam and one on a ship) and the North Vietnam Army receive no more supplies. No more war, no more killing by either side, and the war is over. The Communists lose and the people win – overnight!

Unfortunately, none of this was done. Instead the war dragged on and on and over 47,000 of America's fine young men paid the ultimate price with their lives, with tens of thousands more damaged for life. Chapter Two details how America was actually supplying "both sides" during the war – essentially giving trade and aid to the enemy to kill our soldiers.

Some elitists, ignorant of Communist atrocities, have said that the South Vietnamese are better off now that the Communists have taken over. An "Asian" is more comfortable in that type of government, they say. After the Reds took over, the Vietnamese people indicated otherwise. Thousands risked everything to take off to sea in small boats, knowing their chance of survival and rescue was very small. One lady explained it very simply: "I knew we might all die at sea." Knowing the great danger, why did they risk the flight? Mrs. Ngo answered, "It is better to die at sea than to live under communism."[8] This doesn't really indicate the magnitude of what she was saying. The reality is that they were more willing to be slowly "cooked" to death under a tropical sun at sea than to live under communism. Too bad so many of our U. S. college professors brainwashing our kids don't understand that.

Chart A lists countries that, in most cases, were taken over by the Reds with hardly a shot being fired, as Americans stood by – uninformed and apathetic. There were two exceptions (Korea and Vietnam) where our government was forced by the public outcry to "Do something!" Those results ended in tragedies. This only confirms what Pat Robinson wrote in his 1991 book, *The New World Order:*

> Instead of victory, in Vietnam we played at war and bled our young men to death. We bled our treasury. And worst of all, we bled our national resolve. In Vietnam, the United States was forced by its leaders to suffer the first military loss in its history. Above all else, we showed the world daily that the foreign policy establishment of the United States and its allies would not permit this nation to ever "defeat" communism. **We could struggle against communism; we could arm against communism; but we could not be allowed to win against communism** (Emphasis added).

Who was controlling our never ending disastrous policies? No one is ever held accountable. No doubt, many were involved, but during the Vietnam War, one name has now surfaced as a key player, when a collection of over 2,000 papers was made public by George Washington University's National Security Archive. These recently released papers contained memos and letters written by Henry Kissinger, long time national security advisor and Secretary of State to Presidents Nixon and Ford. The Associated Press summary of the papers said that, "Henry Kissinger acknowledged to [Communist] China in 1972 that the United States could accept a Communist takeover of South Vietnam, if it evolved after a withdrawal of U.S. Forces." The A.P. story also revealed that Kissinger told the Chinese Communist dictator that, the United States respected the North Vietnamese and said, **"We have had no interest in destroying it or even defeating it."**

What is the definition of treason? Can all of these American and Vietnamese lives be sacrificed on the altar of political intrigue and no one is held responsible? Do the surviving wounded soldiers from Vietnam still around in their wheelchairs realize that they were over there fighting a war that the top American official told the enemy we have "no interest in winning?" Unbelievable, but true! Kissinger is still alive and is treated as a dignitary and foreign policy expert by our media. Strange, isn't it?

SIDE NOTE: Reread what Kissinger wrote while our boys were fighting and dying in Vietnam. Today he is still accepted as a expert in foreign affairs, regularly seen on TV. Do you think that is an unusual exception? Sorry, this type of person never changes. They seem to hate America, or at least what they believe America stands for. Recently we had a repeat performance. Only this time they didn't bother to wait 40 years to let it out and when it did come out, the White House willingly agreed. As reported by Fox News (12-19-11): *The White House on Monday defended Vice President Joe Biden for saying that the Taliban* **isn't an enemy of the United States!** *Biden said this despite the years spent fighting that militant Islamic group who gave a home to Al Qaeda and its leader Osama bin Laden while he plotted the September 11 terror attacks.* If the Taliban is not our enemy why are we fighting them and why are innocent American and others dying in the process? What happened after this preposterous statement came out? Nothing!

The list in Chart A also does not include other diplomatic blunders that have caused tremendous additional problems, even to this day. Many people regard Jimmy Carter as the worst President in our history [although many now believe that Obama is replacing him]. But most base that on his disastrous economic policies or on his "giving away" our Panama Canal (incidentally, now controlled by the Chinese Communists). However, much less publicized but far more damaging in the long run was Carter's decision in the late 1970's to undermine the Shah of Iran to help oust him and bring the Ayatollah Khomeini to power. Giving the radical Muslims an entire country as a base in which to operate was a disaster that has had and will continue to have very significant consequences. Instead of having the Shah of Iran, a close friend of America, who was heavily armed and acted as the "policeman on the block" in that treacherous region, we now face a deadly enemy moving quickly towards nuclear weapons. This move by Carter was probably the biggest foreign policy blunder in American history! It is of interest to note that upon being put into power by Carter, the first thing the Ayatollah did to thank him was to humiliate him by taking our Embassy Staff as hostages. Of course, this was not a surprise to students of history. Similar to the Communists when they takeover a country, the first thing they often do is round-up the so-called intellectuals who were their biggest supporters and put them in jail or off to the firing squads. The Communists' reason is simple and logical: "If they are so gullible that even their own country couldn't trust them, why should we?"

The Shah himself confirmed in 1979, what most now accept – that it was Carter who undermined him and put the Islamic terrorists in control of Iran. In Jack Anderson's column of February 13, 1979, he quotes the Shah as stating that it was no mistake or bungling which led the terrorists to takeover. Anderson quotes the Shah as saying, "Carter and the CIA knew all too well what was happening in Iran." In fact the Shah believes the CIA engineered his fall from power and the ascendency of Khomeini. So now the Islamic Jihadists no longer had to work out of caves or tents in the desert. They had an entire, oil rich country to use as their base of operations.

Late in the Carter term when the people around Carter became so blatantly anti-American, it was no surprise to read the "leaked" memo from one of his top men in the National Security Council. Disgracefully, the memo read, "Even if the United States could attain strategic superiority (over the U.S.S.R) it would not be desirable because I suspect we would occasionally use it as a way of throwing our weight around in some very risky ways…. It is in the U.S. interest to allow the few remaining areas of strategic advantages to fade away."[9] Stop and realize the implications of what this top advisor was writing to the President of the United States!

SIDE NOTE: Embracing a recent invitation by the Castro brothers, Jimmy Carter visited Cuba. "We greeted each other as old friends," gushed the former president after his meeting with Fidel Castro. "In 2002, we received him warmly," Fidel reciprocated. "Now I reiterated to him our respect and esteem." "Jimmy Carter was the best of all US presidents," stated Raul Castro, while personally seeing off his American guest. Jimmy Carter earned all of this warmth, esteem and joviality from Cuba's Stalinist rulers by doing everything within his power to dismantle the so-called embargo against them … and yet as president, Mr. Carter imposed more economic sanctions against more nations than any other American president in modern history. These sanctions were against Chile, Iran, Rhodesia, Nicaragua, South Africa, Paraguay and Uruguay. Mr. Carter was extremely selective in imposing his sanctions – let's give him that. He was careful to punish only countries that were US allies at the time![10]

When President Reagan came to power in 1980, the Communist takeovers stopped – worldwide! The reason is simple. Reagan was the first President of either party to really understand communism. When he described the USSR as an "evil empire" the U.S. media became hysterical. He also quickly reversed Carter's disarmament policies, because he believed that peace came through strength, not weakness. By the time Reagan left office in 1988, the Soviet Union was crumbling and the United States was again a mighty military superpower. The Soviets tried to maneuver Reagan into various disarmament treaties that would have saved them, but he refused. Once again the U.S. media went ballistic. In the end, the USSR fell apart as an entity. For over 60 years, America had done nothing to stop the Communist march; rather, at every opportunity, instead of stopping the Soviets, those treacherous individuals or fools working within our midst aided them in every way. When Reagan was asked what his goal had been to cause this total reversal to happen, he replied simply, "We win, they lose." Many astute observers had always believed that communism would fall under its own weight, if we just quit aiding them at every turn. Finally America had a President who understood that simple concept.

Shortly after Reagan left office in 1988, the USSR officially fell. For many people, the days of fearing communism were over. Most Americans forgot that China, with a population of over a billion people, was still a Communist country, not to mention the many smaller countries, also under Communist rule. Also, many henchmen in Russia were still in a place of leadership. All of this was already causing concern among astute American observers.

1990 Ethiopia
1990 Namibia
1996 Belarus
1998 Venezuela (Hugo Chavez)
2005 Bolivia (Eva Morales)
2006 Nicaragua (Daniel Ortega)
2006 Ecuador (Rafael Correa)
2007 Guatemala (Alarvo Colom)
2008 Paraguay (Fernando Lugo)
2008 Honduras (Manuel Zelaya)
2009 El Salvador (Mauricio Funes)
2011 Brazil (Dilma Rousseff)
2011 Peru (Ollanta Humala)

CHART B
Countries Moving into the Socialist and/or Communist Orbits and Approximate Dates

Chart B above lists the countries that have been swept into the Socialist and/or Communist orbit after President Reagan left office in 1988. During this latter period the methods of "takeovers" have changed. Using the cover of "Liberation Theology" and promising to improve living conditions, they have moved into numerous Central and South American countries through elections. Once voted in, they have moved in a more predictable pattern of suppressing freedoms and consolidating their power. A new pattern has also occurred in the African countries listed. The dates are not as specific as those listed in Chart A, as the election of progressives gives a semblance of democracy at first, only to see the grim reality as time goes on. In some cases the countries have moved in and out of dictatorships. Many would argue that some of these are simply Socialist regimes and have no relation to the Communist governments. It is then very important at this point to quote a leading Communist on this subject:

John Strachey was a prominent member of the Labor Party of Great Britain in the 1950's. He openly acknowledged he was a Communist. He wrote the benchmark book entitled, *The Theory and Practice of Socialism*. In the book he clearly acknowledged that, "it is impossible to establish communism as the immediate successor to capitalism. It is accordingly proposed to establish socialism as something that can be put in place of our present decaying capitalism. **Hence, Communists work for the establishment of socialism as a necessary transition stage on the road to communism**" (emphasis added).

We here in America need to keep that important concept in mind as we move closer and closer to a Socialist state. How will this end?

Names of the current leaders of the countries listed in Chart B are put in parentheses, so you can follow the news reports and know whom to watch. Just how "Red" each of these leaders is can be gauged on how often they are in Cuba, visiting with Fidel.

References

None Dare Call It Treason ... 25 Years Later, John Stormer, (Paperback Edition), Liberty Bell Press, 1992
Shadow World, Robert Chandler, Regnery Co. , 2008.
Kissinger on the Couch, Phyllis Schlafly and Chester Ward, 1975.
Witness, Whittaker Chambers, 1952.

**Current issues are covered daily by Glenn Beck on: GBTV.com.

Chapter One Notes

1. reformed-theology.org/html/books/best_enemy/ conclusions.htm
2. Ambassador William C. Bullitt, *Life Magazine*, August 23, 1948.
3. *St. Petersburg Times*, March 30, 2008.
4. Associated Press, June 22, 1979.
5. United Press International, September 3, 1978.
6. Film: *Communist Encirclement 1961,* NEP, Harding College.
7. *Tampa Tribune*, March 13, 1968, Pg. 6-B, General Ira Eaker.
8. *U.S.N.W.R.*, November 1975, Pg. 53.
9. *U.S.N.W.R.,* February 1979, Victor Utgoff.
10. *The Schwarz Report*, July 2011.

CHAPTER TWO

Goal No. 4: Permit free trade between all nations regardless of Communist affiliation and regardless of whether or not items could be used for war.
Goal No. 5: Extension of long-term loans to Russia and Soviet satellites.
Goal No. 6: Provide American aid to all nations regardless of Communist domination.

Many knowledgeable students of the Cold War era felt that if America just quit supplying foreign aid and trade to the Communist countries, the Soviet Empire would crumble on its own. We wouldn't have to do anything on the offensive – just quit helping them as they were trying to destroy us. Yet, instead, we went all out in every way to keep the Red Block supplied. While doing this, we were spending billions of dollars on national defense to protect ourselves against these same countries. It is as if the State Department had one policy and the Defense Department had a totally different evaluation. Since we now know that most of the Soviet spies were concentrated in our State Department, it is tragic – but it does make sense. All of this foolishness (treason) started when President Roosevelt gave diplomatic recognition to Russia in 1933. That was well before the Soviets became our "allies" against Nazi Germany during WWII. In 1933 there was no excuse for America to do this for a Communist Dictatorship that had already exposed itself as totally evil, exterminating millions of its own citizens under the vicious Stalin regime. This recognition by the U.S. allowed the criminal Russian government to obtain monetary credit and to set up embassies around the world – the main purpose of which would be to allow them to use those embassies for espionage purposes. Once WWII broke out, the Soviets then had the incredibly "good fortune" to become our allies. With that as an excuse, the State Department opened the floodgates to supply the Reds. To summarize a portion of this tragic era in the early days, another section of Skousen's book *The Naked Communist* is reproduced at length below. It documents how devastating this early policy was for America's future:

> The Story of American Lend-Lease to Russia
>
> This American policy of generosity immediately began to manifest itself. Billions of dollars of Russian Lend-Lease were authorized. Even the deliberate sacrifice of American self-interest was evident in some of the orders received by U.S. military services. An order to the Air Service Command dated January l, 1943, carried this astounding mandate: "The modification, equipment, and movement of Russian planes have been given first priority, even over planes for the U.S. Army Air Forces."
>
> The U.S. Congress was not quite as enthusiastic toward Russia as the diplomatic strategists. Congress specifically restricted Russian Lend-Lease to materials to be used for military action against the Axis enemy. It forbade the shipment of materials which would be used for civilian personnel or the rehabilitation of Russia after the war. This was in no way designed to show unfriendliness toward the Russian people. It was simply an expression of belief that U.S. resources should not be used to promote Communist Russia into a world power. Someday the Russian people would perhaps regain power. Some day the Russian people would perhaps regain their freedom, and that would be the time to share resources. Meanwhile, non-military generosity would only strength the post-war position of the Communist dictatorship. In spite of these legal restrictions, however, the uninhibited generosity of the diplomats dominated Lend-Lease rather than Congress or the leaders of the Military.

General John R. Deane, for example, who was in Moscow as chief of the U.S Military Mission turned down a request for 25 large 200-horsepower Diesel marine engines because the engines already sent to Russia were rusting in open storage and from all appearances were simply being stockpiled for post-war use. Furthermore, the engines were badly needed by General MacArthur in the South Pacific. After hearing General Deane's decision, the Russians appealed to Harry Hopkins (head of the Lend-Lease program) who overruled General Deane. During the following two years a total of 1,305 of these engines were sent to Russia at a cost to the American people of $30,745,947.

After Pearl Harbor, when Navy officials were given the highest possible priority for copper wire to be used in the repair of U.S. battleships, they found the Russians had an even higher priority for an order of copper wire which was apparently to be used for post-war rehabilitation of Russian cities. The wire was turned over to the Russians in such quantities that it had to be stored on a 20-acre lot in Westchester County, New York, where it remained until the war was nearly over. A few months before the Armistice, it was shipped to Russia for the rehabilitation of their communications systems.

Since the close of World War II, the American people have gradually learned the details concerning the flood of goods and treasure which went to Russia under LendLease. The lists which have been published are from Russian records. They were secured by an American officer, Major George Racey Jordan, who was the official U.S. expediter for Russian Lend-Lease at the Great Falls Air Base in Montana. An analysis of these lists showed that according to Russian records, the Communists received over eleven billion dollars worth of Lend-Lease and that in spite of the legal restrictions against it, the diplomatic strategists included $3,040,423,000 worth of American goods, paid for by American taxpayers, which definitely does not appear to be authorized by the Lend-Lease act. These lists show shipments of vast stockpiles of "non-munitions" chemicals together with voluminous shipments of cigarette cases, phonograph records, ladies' compacts, sheet music, pianos, antique furniture, $388,844 worth of "notions and cheap novelties," women's jewelry, household furnishings, fishing tackle, lipstick, perfumes, dolls, bank vaults, playground equipment, and quantities of many other types of illegal, non-military merchandise.

Students of Russian wartime history point out that American Lend-Lease began feeding into Russia at a time when she was almost prostrate. She had lost most of her crops as a result of the scorched earth campaign designed to slow Nazi advances. Even with Lend-Lease food the troops had to be rationed at a bare subsistence level so it is likely that without Lend-Lease the Russian resistance might well have collapsed. Furthermore, the German occupation cut the Russians off from many of their major industrial centers. In addition to U.S. planes, munitions, chemicals, tools, heavy machinery, and so forth, the amazing American "Arsenal of Democracy" provided Russia with 478,899 motor vehicles. This was nearly half of all motor vehicles used on the Soviet front.

It is an interesting commentary on the Communist psychology to note that the United States never received an official "thank you" from Russia for the eleven billion dollars worth of Lend-Lease goods which were paid for and literally "donated" to the Communist Motherland by the American people. Stalin's excuse was that his government felt the United States made an error when it stopped Lend-Lease at the close of the war. He made it icy clear that under the circumstances his people did not feel an expression of gratitude would be either appropriate or justifiable.

Russian Attempts to Secure the Secrets of the Atomic Bomb

Throughout World War II Russian espionage vigorously concentrated on the most important thing to come out of the War – the harnessing of atomic energy. A twopronged thrust was employed to get the information as it was developed: one by espionage and the other by diplomatic channels. For a time the diplomatic channels were particularly productive, not only for atomic energy secrets, but for all military and industrial information.

Major Jordan first became aware of this at the Great Falls Lend-Lease Air Base when the Russians began bringing large quantities of cheap, black suitcases along with them whenever they left the United States. They refused to let Jordan see the contents of the grounds that the suitcases were pieces of "diplomatic luggage" and therefore immune to inspection. One night the Russian commander at the base almost demanded that Jordan go into Great Falls as his dinner guest. Jordan was suspicious but accepted. About midnight he received an excited call that a plane had just landed and the Soviets were going to take off for Russia without waiting for Jordan's clearance. Jordan raced back to the airfield. Sure enough, the plane was a joker. In it were fifty black suitcases protected by armed Russian guards. Jordan ordered a GI to hold the guards at bay and to shoot to kill if they forcibly interfered with his inspection.

Jordan later testified under oath before a congressional committee that he found each suitcase to contain a file of information about U.S. industry, harbors, troops, railroads, communications, and so forth. In one suitcase Jordan said he found a letter on White House stationery signed by Harry Hopkins and addressed to the number three man in the Russian hierarchy. Attached to the letter was a map of the top-secret Manhattan (atomic energy) Project, together with descriptive data detailing with atomic energy experiments! One folder in this suitcase had written on it, "From Hiss." At the time Jordan did not know who Hiss was. Inside the folder were numerous military documents. Another folder contained Department of State documents. Some of these were letters from the U.S embassy in Moscow giving confidential evaluations of the Russian situation and detailed analytical impressions of Russian officials. Now they were being secretly shipped back for the Russians to read. When Major Jordan reported the facts to Washington he was severely criticized for holding up the plane!

In April, 1943, the Russian liaison officer told Jordan that a very special shipment of experimental chemicals was coming through. The Russian officer called Harry Hopkins in Washington and then turned the phone over to Jordan. Major Jordan reports that Harry Hopkins told him: "I don't want you to discuss this with anyone, and it is not to go on the records. Don't make a big production of it, but just send it through quietly, in a hurry." The Russian officer later told Jordan the shipment was "bomb powder" and Jordan saw an entry in the officer's folder which said "Uranium." The shipment came through June 10, 1943. It was the first of several. At least

1,465 pounds of uranium salts are said to have been sent through to the Soviet Union. Metallurgists estimate that this could be reduced to 6.25 pounds of fissionable U-235. This is two pounds more than would be necessary to produce an atomic explosion.

On July 24, 1945, at Potsdam, President Truman announced to Winston Churchill and Joseph Stalin that the United States had finally developed a highly secret bomb. He told them this bomb possessed almost unbelievable explosive power. Secretary of State James F. Byrnes was watching Stalin and noted that he did not seem particularly surprised nor even interested in the announcement.

Four years later (September 23, 1949), President Truman announced to the world that Russia had successfully exploded an atomic bomb – years ahead of U.S. expectations! Some informed officials wondered why, with all the help they received, the Russians had not exploded one long before.

This area of trade and aid offers the opportunity to document hypocrisy (treason?) at its worst. As of 2011, it is illegal to trade or in many cases to even visit countries like North Korea, Cuba and others. Why? The official answer is because they are evil Communist counties – our enemies. Sounds logical; however, where do a vast majority of all of our goods come from that are presently shipped into America? Communist China, of course. The Communist leaders in China, have by expert estimates (R. J. Rummel, *Death by Government*) murdered in cold blood over 75,000,000 of their own people. So, it is legal to trade with **them**, but not with Cuba? Yes, Castro is a bad guy too, but you get the point. It is all political. No rhyme or reason – except to those that know "The Goals."

A case can be built to show how this trade imbalance is undermining our entire work force. American workers cannot be expected to compete with goods produced in China by slave labor. Yet the unions, supposedly created to protect the worker, continue to support the politicians who allow this to continue. How does anyone expect an American worker to produce a competitively priced product, when their Chinese counterpart in many cases is literally a slave or in the best case, is working for a few dollars a day?

Books and articles have abundantly documented that Goals 4, 5 and 6 have been accomplished, far beyond the original expectations of the Communists. Our direct aid (giveaways) to enemy countries has been ongoing for decades, with no end in sight.

A graphic illustration of how far these Goals have been accomplished can be found by studying how our aid and trade policies worked even during a "shooting war" with the Communists in Vietnam! A summary of this total lunacy is detailed below [lengthy excerpts taken from the book, *Death of a Nation*, by John Stormer]:

> As American soldiers died in Vietnam, America's leaders in Washington increased America's trade with the Soviet Union and her satellites. The expanded U.S. program helped to build up the Communist industrial machine, which supplied 80% of the guns and bullets used against Americans in Vietnam. Why does the U.S. regularly bail the Communists out of their economic difficulties with aid and trade? Whenever the Communists admit they are falling behind the West in a key area, the U.S. provides aid. For example, on February 24, 1965 the Soviet newspaper *Pravda* called for – importation by the Russians of large amounts of Western computers and technical know-how to make up for a serious lag in certain aspects of Russian computer development. In less than a month, the U.S. Department of Commerce licensed exports of
>
> 41 shipments of electronic computer equipment to the Communist countries of Eastern Europe, despite their potential for bolstering the Communist war machine. As one newspaper pointed out, computers may be used interchangeably on weapons design and manufacture, other scientific and technological problem solving, and a vast number of non-military applications.
>
> This is not an isolated case. As American boys fought and died in Vietnam, the government in Washington arranged for American companies to sell to the Communist nations radio communication equipment, rocket engines, synthetic rubber, synthetic fibers, containers for explosives, computers, nuclear radiation and detection devices, fertilizer, chemicals, combustion engines, industrial processing control instruments, and various other products which

build their war potential. The United States also regularly helps the Communists to keep up with the West technologically. For example:

Under the 1966 Cultural Exchange Agreement, Soviet scientific teams were given the right to visit and probe deeply into such highly technical and vital installations as telephone and electronic facilities, gas and water treatment plants, high voltage electrical power transmission facilities, metallurgical laboratories, and plants producing chemicals and agricultural machinery. To make it easier for Soviet scientists to evaluate certain U.S. Air Force research reports, they were printed with a Russian language summary included.

Congressman Glen Lipscomb (R-Cal), who exposed the practice, called the inclusion of the Russian language summaries in reports paid for by American taxpayers "incredible, but true!" American taxpayers have also paid the bill for special training of Communist nuclear scientists in the United States. Under the headline, "TaxPaid Spies?" the Indianapolis News said: Five scientists from Communist-ruled Poland will have their nuclear research studies in the United States subsidized by the tax-supported National Science Foundation. The NSF has offered each of them grants ranging from $14,760 to $16,160 to travel in the United States and engage in research concerning high energy physics. In this work, they would have access to the Atomic Energy Commission's Brookhaven and Argonne Laboratories.

In commenting on the arrival of the first of the Polish nuclear scientist-spies, Congressman Richard Roudebush (R-Ind) said: "Only this past weekend the Communist government of Poland announced a mammoth demonstration to show support of the Communist cause in Vietnam. It's an incredible situation when during a time of war our government admits scientists from a nation allied with our foe in Vietnam." The usually very liberal executive council of the AFL-CIO recognizes the fallacy of Americans helping to build up the Communist industrial machine. Meeting in Miami, Florida in March 1965, the council said: "The Communists seek U.S. trade only to help overcome the serious economic difficulties while continuing to build up their arsenal of nuclear weapons. Such help by American and other business interests can only finance and facilitate further Soviet aggressions against the democracies."

The Johnson Administration – which the AFL-CIO sent to Washington – and continues to support has arranged, promoted and encouraged the trade with the enemy by American business. Washington will continue to do so until the people of America – and organizations like the AFL-CIO – stop electing Congressmen who favor aid and trade to the enemy. Efforts to stop foreign aid to the Communists have regularly been defeated in Congress. On November 8, 1967, Congressman H. R. Gross (R-Iowa) tried to amend the foreign aid bill to prohibit any aid to nations which trade with North Vietnam. Congress defeated the amendment by a vote of 200 to 196.

If during wartime, we directly aided and traded with an enemy who is supplying products to countries killing our own soldiers, the excuses and rationale have no real meaning, other than the obvious fact that those making decisions here in the U.S. do not have our best interest at heart. Today trading with certain Communist countries is accepted and encouraged as normal, but the people blazing this trail during wartime have never been held accountable. Now we even give direct aid to China! Think of that – aid to a Communist country from whom we are forced to **borrow** hundreds of billions of dollars. Insane! Unfortunately, Goals 4 and 6 have long since been totally accomplished! As far as Goal 5 is concerned, we didn't bother with long-term *loans*, in most cases we just gave it away – to our enemies – even in wartime! Is it insanity or is it treason?

References
The China Threat, Bill Gertz, Regnery Co., 2002.
Mao: The Untold Story, Jung Chang and John Halliday, Knopf, 2006.

CHAPTER THREE

Goal No. 7: Grant recognition of Red China. Admission of Red China into the U.N.

On October 25, 1971, Communist China was granted full membership into the United Nations and further, given a seat on the powerful Security Council (with veto power). To rub it in, at the same time, in an unprecedented move with no legal basis, our friend and former wartime ally Nationalist China, now referred to as Taiwan, was removed from the U.N. altogether (so as not to offend the Communists). It is pertinent to note that no other country has ever been thrown out of the U.N!

On January 1, 1979, the United States formally gave diplomatic recognition to Red China as the official government of China.

Both specific items accomplished! Most Americans now do not realize the historical significances of those two events. The entire China saga is a rather long and tragic story. The details have been fully documented in several important books. To briefly summarize, our country and China were close allies in WWII against Japan. After the war, internal Communist agitators began to organize and propagandize against the existing Chinese Nationalist government under Chiang Kai-shek. As had happened so many times, before and since, the U.S. media and various politicians began to pick up on the propaganda war against the pro-American Chinese government. Slowly in the American media, the Communist agitator Mao Tse-Tung began being described as an agrarian reformer, instead of a Communist. At the same time our wartime ally Chiang Kai-shek, who was then the President of China, was being undermined as an "evil dictator" who needed to be replaced. After the U.S. State Department got involved, the situation got worse. Several of the U.S. government officials in charge of determining what our policy should be were later exposed as secret Communist agents, working under the direction of Moscow. Because of the American policies, the Communists were able to takeover all of China in 1949 and Chiang had to flee with his Army to the island of Taiwan. The State Department had crippled the Chiang forces by stopping all arms aid to him, while supplies flowed freely to the Reds. The **Judiciary Committee of the U.S. Senate** investigated all of the charges and counter-charges and issued a full report which stated that: **We find a conspiracy, Communist-inspired, that led to American defeat. High American officials were duped. Policies were influenced that gave the Communists their greatest victory. The loss of China, after defeat of Japan, represents the greatest defeat in U.S. history.** [1]

As usual most Americans didn't follow the details of this Report and the media covered-up this explosive story, since much of the pro-Mao and anti-Chiang propaganda was pushed by the U.S. Press to begin with. However, a few in Washington were aroused by the Committee's shocking report. John F. Kennedy, then a U.S. Congressman (later our 35th President), spoke out most forcefully, as recorded in the Congressional Record of February 21, 1949: "Over these past few days we have learned the extent of the disasters befalling China. Our policy in China has reaped the whirlwind. The continued insistence that aid would not be forthcoming unless a coalition government with the Communists was formed was a crippling blow to the Nationalist government (of Chiang Kai-shek). This is the tragic story of China whose freedom we once fought to preserve. **What our young men had saved, our diplomats and our President have frittered away.**"

It is very significant to note the particular President that Congressman Kennedy was referring to was his fellow Democrat, Harry S. Truman. Having risked his own life fighting in the Pacific theater of the war to save China's freedom, Kennedy was more interested in the truth being exposed, than in disastrous, partisan, political cover-ups.

Reference
How the Far East was Lost, Anthony Kubeck, Regnery Co. 1963.

Chapter Three Note
1. Film: *Communist Encirclement, 1961*, National Educational Program, Harding College.

CHAPTER FOUR

Goal No. 11: Promote the U.N. as the only hope for mankind.

Many books have been written to show the disaster the U.N. has been for America. The easiest way to briefly summarize this topic in a very convincing manner is to simply remind the reader that Alger Hiss was the first acting secretary-general of the United Nations Charter Conference in 1945. He was the head of the committee that set up the whole apparatus. For those who are not familiar with the name of Alger Hiss, they need only to be told that he was proven to be an undercover Soviet agent working as a traitor within our government. It is not too difficult to imagine then that the U.S.S.R. was very interested in promoting the U.N., since "their man" was the one who organized the Charter and consequentially, the way the U.N. works and the way it is run. It seemed logical to most Americans that the U.N. was a great idea – a chance for various ideas to be expressed and discussed – "Better to talk than to fight." Unfortunately, the devil was in the details.

What the Reds did to capitalize on all of the various international organizations created after the end of WWII is unbelievable! The world has never worked the same since. They never missed an opportunity. The U.N. was not the only organization our enemies manipulated to their advantage. At the Bretton Woods Monetary Conference in 1944, the International Monetary Fund and the World Bank were both created.

Harry Dexter White and John Maynard Keynes
Figure 2

The photo in Figure 2 shows the American Communist traitor Harry Dexter White (who regularly advised President Roosevelt and Truman in various capacities) chatting with John Maynard Keynes (on the right), a long time leading Socialist member of the Fabian Society. These two were instrumental in guiding all major decisions at the Monetary Conference!

Think of it! All of the World Organizations that have so much influence on our country and our lives were all formed and constructed by our enemies. Yet few know.

See the **Agenda 21 Project** web sites given below. A whole, new monster is being created. Start watching for the buzz-words, "sustainable development" and you will see them every where, being applied to every situation.

References
The Fearful Master, G. Edward Griffin, Western Island, 1964. (About the origins of the U.N.)
Surrender is not an Option, John Bolton, Threshold Editions, 2008. (About how the U.N. is working in recent times)
Keynes at Harvard, Zygmund Dobbs, 1969.
Fabian Freeway, Rose L. Martin, 1966.

Web Addresses (Concerning the U.N. Agenda 21 Project)
www.sovereignty.net, www.freedomadvocates.org

CHAPTER FIVE

Goal No. 12: Resist any attempt to outlaw the Communist Party.
Goal No. 13: Do away with all loyalty oaths.

It is not the American constitutional way to "outlaw" political parties. But the Communists wanted to be vigilant and make sure that it never did happen, as they became more vocal and open in America. Of course they have been successful in this effort. Some would argue that the Communist Party is not a political party at all, but rather a tool being used by a foreign government.

As for loyalty oaths, that is a different story. Outlawing a political party is one thing, but simply requiring people who work for the government to be loyal to that government is not an unreasonable request. In other words, protest all you want, but if you are going to be paid with government funds, you need to pledge that you are not a spy or a traitor. One doesn't have to believe every government policy is correct, but only assert that they are not undercover agents, loyal to an enemy government. This topic isn't even discussed anymore, much less enforced.

References
Treason, Ann Coulter, Crown Forum, 2003.
The Soviet World of American Communism, Harvey Klehr and John Earl Hayes. Yale University Press, 1998.

CHAPTER SIX

Goal No. 14: Continue giving Russia access to the U.S. Patent Office.

It is no longer a question of giving Russia access to our Patent Office, but now the radicals want to totally undermine our country by changing almost everything in our patent law system that has kept America at the forefront of innovation. Phyllis Schlafly summarized their efforts in her Eagle Forum Newsletter of July 30, 2007. (The bill she is referring to did not succeed at that time, but has been brought back again and again.) Her commentary is an excellent summary of the situation and examines the horrible repercussions of such bills that are still being relentlessly pushed in Congress:

> In extraordinary coordination, the judiciary committees of both the U.S. Senate and House of Representatives in the same week approved a bill, which, if it becomes law, will spell the end of America's world leadership in innovation.
>
> Called the Patent Reform Act, it is a direct attack on the unique and successful patent system created by the U.S. Constitution. Before 1999, the U.S. Patent Office was required to keep secret the contents of a patent application until a patent was granted, and to return the application in secret to the inventor if a patent was denied. That protected the legal rights of the inventor, who could then go back to the drawing board to perfect his invention and try again.

A mischievous congressional "reform" in 1999 authorized the U.S. Patent Office to shift to the Japanese and European practice of publishing patent applications 18 months after filing whether or not a decision is yet made on granting a patent. Congress allowed a patent application, under certain conditions, to be exempt from the publication requirement, but the default procedure is to publish.

The 2007 Patent bill would delete this exemption and require publication of all patent applications 18 months after filing regardless of whether a decision has been made on granting a patent.

By 2006, the U.S. Patent Office had placed 1,271,000 patent applications on the Internet, giving access to anyone anywhere in the world. This foolish practice created a gold mine for China to steal U.S. innovations and get to market quickly.

Chinese pirates don't roam the high seas looking for booty but sit at their computers, roam the Internet, and steal the details of U.S. inventions that the U.S. Patent Office loads online. This practice became China's research and development program, and it is even more efficient than China's network of industrial and military spies. U.S. policy has always been to grant a patent to the first one who actually invents something. But the new patent bill would change to the foreign system, which grants patents to the first one to file papers.

First-to-file would be a windfall to mega corporations and a big disadvantage to the small-entity inventor. Firstto-file would invite an avalanche of applications from the big companies that have the resources to grind out multiple filings, and the small inventor would be lost in the shuffle. The new patent bill offers yet another way for patent pirates to steal U.S. technology. It's called postgrant review: a plan to make it easier to challenge patents during the entire life of the patent.

Another provision of the new patent bill would shift decision-making about damages for patent infringement from market valuations to judgments by judges and juries. This would increase litigation and limit the ability of independent inventors and small companies to enforce their rights or to win just compensation from those who infringe their rights. The new bill would also transfer unprecedented rule-making authority to the Patent office. That's an abdication of congressional responsibility. Add it all up, and it is clear that the new patent bill is a big attack on the constitutional property rights of individual inventors and small enterprises, the very kind of entrepreneurs who give us our most important innovations. About a third of all patent applications are filed by individual inventors, small companies, universities, and nonprofit groups. The common thread in the changes to be made by the new patent bill is that they favor big companies like Microsoft and hurt individual and small-entity inventors.

Microsoft has thousands of patents, and recently argued that the free GNU/Linux operating system infringes over 200 of them. Microsoft wants to be able to use its huge patent portfolio to intimidate potential competitors, and at the same time it wants it to be easier to knock out individual patents.

If Congress wants to do something constructive for our patent system, Congress should reinstate the rule that the Patent Office may not publish a patent application until a patent is granted, and if it is denied the application must be returned to the inventor with his secrets intact. Congress should also give back to the Patent Office the flow of fees paid by inventors, which Congress took away in 1999 to spend on other projects. Then the Patent Office can hire more examiners and reduce its backlog of 800,000 applications. The U.S. patent system is the vital factor in the technological lead that gives the United States an edge over competitors and enemies.

It is very clear that the trend in this direction far surpasses Mr. Skousen's worst fears.

CHAPTER SEVEN

Goal No. 15: Capture one or both of the political parties in the United States.

Mr. Skousen was probably aware that this Goal was well on its way to completion, even before he listed it. He apparently did not want the importance of his other material to be discredited by what some would perceive to be partisan political comments or conclusions. As with most of these Goals, many books have been written to prove the issue being discussed. Pertaining to this specific Goal, there are dozens of books now in print to prove this point and need not be belabored here. As previously mentioned, the intent of this book is to simply illustrate that a book published over fifty years ago predicted all of these happenings and further show that the prime moving force behind the pushing of these Goals was the world-wide Communist network, assisted by their American Marxist collaborators, progressives and dupes.

Even as far back as the 1930's, President Franklin Roosevelt reportedly told a concerned Congressman that, "… there is nothing wrong with the Communists in this country. Several of my best friends are Communists."[1] Following WWII when the Cold War broke out with the Communists, no politician would have dared say anything like that. Yet as has already been documented, the behind the scenes treachery has continued. Ann Coulter's book, *TREASON*, basically proves that a majority of the Democrat Party has been "soft on communism" for decades. The fact of the matter is, other than Reagan, the Republicans didn't do much better in this life and death struggle.

Now in 2011, we have a President who apparently agrees with Roosevelt and also has "best friends" who are Communists[2]. President Obama has openly appointed Communists and Marxists to positions in his administration (Van Jones the most prominent). As for the Congress, in 2009 over 80 members belonged to the Congressional Progressive Caucus. Of the twenty House Committees; eleven were chaired by the Caucus members. The Caucus is as openly Socialist as could be in America.

The strangest part of this is that the Radicals that are in the White House don't seem to try and hide their allegiance anymore. White House Communications Director, Anita Dunn openly bragged in a speech[3] given to a high school graduating class that one of her favorite political philosophers was Mao Tse Tung, the brutal Communist dictator of China responsible for the mass murdering of tens of millions of his own people. What are they thinking when they tell this to our next generation? Are these people living in a parallel universe? Or are they so arrogant that they don't care? Of course they do know that they can count on the mainstream media giving them a pass on all of this.

To get an overview of just how effective President Obama and the Democrats have been in aiding in the accomplishment of this Goal, a letter I wrote to the newspaper summarizes the situation as of 2010:

January 24, 2010

St. Petersburg Times

Letters to the Editor:

It was refreshing to read the candor in your lead editorial of January 24th concerning President Obama's "Productive Two Years." Most knowledgeable liberals and liberal organizations have been very quiet on this subject, while the less informed liberal groups have been howling over President Obama "compromising" with the Republicans on the modest tax cut agreement and not closing Guantanamo. As I shall attempt to summarize, President Obama has already accomplished more "fundamental change" (as he promised) in two years than FDR did in four terms.

The complaining on both sided has provided the "cover" needed for Obama to almost complete his massive goal. During his brief time, the government has taken at least partial control of:

1) The Auto Industry [GM & Chrysler].
2) The Financial Industry – all of it.
3) The Entire Healthcare Industry.
4) The Housing Industry.
5) The Student Loan Program.
6) The Food Supply.

In addition, this Administration has prompted basic changes to our American way of life as seen by:

7) The ability to control all businesses by allowing the EPA edicts (that strangle business) to stand as law, without any Congressional input.
8) The ability to control the Internet by FCC edicts, not Congressional actions.
9) Allowing homosexuals to openly serve in the Armed Forces, breaking over 200 years of tradition.
10) Soon on the horizon will be the application of the so-called Fairness Doctrine, to undermine Fox News and all of Talk Radio.

The Federal Government has always had the constitutional authority to control the military, which is a large part of our budget. They have always had indirect control of our money supply, interest rates and inflation – which affects everything. In addition, the Federal Government has indirect control over the price of oil and gas. Adding to all of this is the unbelievable fact that here in the land of *Private Property*, the state and federal governments own 40% of all of our land! Why?

After two years of Obama, the obvious question now is: *What's left?* The answer is: *Almost nothing!* Think about that. The Federal Government now has almost total control over every aspect of our lives and will soon be able to silence all of the voices of information or opposition.

Each of the ten items listed above have been publicized. The problem is most Americans don't correlate the news items as they develop. Many get upset in a certain area, but by the time the next item comes along, they don't relate it to the last one – to see the overall picture of the total transformation taking place. Most are too busy with their jobs or family and their own lives.

If Obama gets a second term, we are finished!

James C. Bowers.

The above letter is my summary. An equally revealing summary from an independent source is given by Norman Podhoretz in the *Wall Street Journal* (August 13, 2011). Because of copyright laws it cannot be reproduced here, but can be found with a Google search. It is well worth the effort! It is really unbelievable and unprecedented that an article so blunt would ever be written in such a reputable publication about a sitting President. It lets one know how bad the situation is and how frightened even mainstream authorities have become.

Finally, I'll conclude this Chapter with some other revealing quotes from a variety of sources. Think carefully about what you are reading and who is saying it:

"The left can and should advance its own views and disagree with the Obama Administration without being disagreeable. Its tone should be respectful. **We are speaking to a friend.**"

Sam Webb – National Chairman, Communist Party USA

"You never want a serious crisis to go to waste. This crisis (the present financial situation) provides us with the opportunity to do things **you could not do before.**"

Rahm Emanuel – President Obama's Chief Staff

"It must be said that, like the breaking of a great dam, the American descent into Marxism is happening with breathtaking speed, against the backdrop of a passive, hapless sheeple – excuse me dear reader – I meant people."

Stanislav Mishin, writing in PRAVDA
(the Russian state newspaper), June 1, 2009

SIDE NOTE: It is interesting to observe a dilemma many liberals have. Their ultimate hero is John F. Kennedy and their ultimate villain is Sen. Joe McCarthy. However, the fact is that Kennedy was himself the most anti-Communist president we have had until Reagan. Unfortunately, all of the Democrat progressives surrounding Kennedy were influencing and redirecting many of his policies. In addition, as we have later learned, President Kennedy was constantly being heavily medicated for pain (Was he also being manipulated and controlled by medication?). The dilemma for liberals is that all of the Kennedy Clan were close friends and admirers of Sen. McCarthy.

As documented on the website, **mcadams.posc.mu.edu/progjfk2.htm:** JFK liked the fact that McCarthy went after the "elites" in the State Department whom JFK regarded with contempt. Even before McCarthy made accusations against the State Department of subversion, JFK had already aligned himself with the militant anti-Communists who blamed the Truman State Department for the "loss" of China, as JFK declared on the House floor in 1949.

There were also other deep personal bonds between JFK and McCarthy by the time McCarthy reached the peak of his power in 1952 and 1953. Not only had McCarthy been a frequent guest at the Kennedy compound in Hyannis, but McCarthy had also dated two Kennedy sisters. The ties with Bobby were forged when he gave RFK a job as minority counsel to his Senate committee investigating domestic communism. RFK would maintain a deep loyalty to a man he loved enough to make him the godfather of his first child.

JFK's warmth for McCarthy was not as great as Bobby's, but he still felt enough of McCarthy to "walk out" at the 100th Anniversary of the Harvard Spree Club dinner. Robert Armory, who had been at the dinner and who later worked in the Kennedy Administration recalled in an oral history at the JFK Library that when a speaker had likened McCarthy to the convicted Soviet spy Alger Hiss, JFK rose to his feet and declared **"How dare you couple the name of a great American patriot with that of a traitor!"** and walked out. The incident has never been denied by anyone who was there, and is accepted by JFK biographers Herbert Parmet, Thomas Reeves and Chris Matthews, (Emphasis added).

The lengthy title of David Horowitz's 2006 book tells it all, and think about it, it was published even before Obama brought all of his radical friends and connections into power. The book's title is: *THE SHADOW PARTY – How George Soros, Hillary Clinton and the Sixties Radicals seized control of the Democrat Party.* Enough said!

Reference Books
The Blueprint, Ken Blackwell, 2010.
The Manchurian President, Aaron Klein, 2010.
You Can Still Trust the Communist (to be Communists), Fred Schwarz and David Noebel, 2010.

Chapter Seven Notes
1. *New York Times*, May 6, 1933.
2. *The Obama Nation*, 2008, Simon & Schuster, Jerome R. Corsi.
3. YouTube.

CHAPTER EIGHT

Goal No. 16: Use technical decisions of the courts to weaken basic American institutions by claiming their activities violate civil rights.

This topic is so massive in scope, that it is impossible to summarize in a Chapter. There are also endless "offshoot" issues involved. Therefore, the reader is referred to the list of books given in the Reference Section below, to pursue whatever aspect of this subject might be of special interest. To claim that this Goal has been accomplished, is a vast understatement! Even after electing a black President, the racial issue continues to be a constant weapon used by liberals. Anyone disagreeing with almost any liberal policy is labeled as a racist.

References
Andrew Kull, *The Color Blind Constitution* (Cambridge Harvard University Press 1992).
Edward Erler, *The Future of Civil Rights*, Notre Dame Journal of Law, Ethics, and Public Policy.
Hugh Davis Graham, *The Civil Rights Era: Origins and Development of National Policy*, 1960-1972 (New York: Oxford University Press).
Herman Belz, Equality Transformed: *A Quarter Century of Affirmative Action* (New Brunswick, NJ: Transaction, 1991).

Nathan Glazer, *Ethnic Dilemmas,* 1964-1982 (Cambridge: Harvard University Press, 1983).

Bayard Rustin, From Protest to Policies *The Future of the Civil Rights Movement,* Commentary, 39 (February 1965).

John Fonte, *Why There is a Culture War: Gramsci and Tocqueville in America*, Policy Review, 104 (December 2000/January 2001).

Ward Connerly, *Created Equal: My Fight Against Race Preferences* (San Francisco: Encounter Books, 2000).

Seymour Martin Lipset, *Equal Chances Versus Equal Results*, Annals of the American Academy of Political and Social Science, 523 (September 1992).

Seymour Martin Lipset, *Affirmative Action and the American Creed*, Washington Post, October 11, 1995.

CHAPTER NINE

Goal No. 17: Get control of the schools. Use them as transmission belts for socialism and current Communist propaganda. Soften the curriculum. Get control of teachers' associations. Put the party line in text-books.

In the 1950's, in most parts of the country, this Goal was unthinkable. The kids walked to the school, as it was a small, decentralized school in the neighborhood. The school teachers were your neighbors. The local school board members were also your neighbors and everyone was working towards the same goal – giving your kids the best education possible.

How much has changed! Now many kids are carted in buses all over town. The schools are larger and centralized. The school board control has been replaced by federal government control, the teachers are now mostly faithful to their radical left-wing National Education Association (NEA) union – not to the kids or parents. This is forcefully exposed in the awardwinning documentary, **Waiting for Superman** (Available on DVD). The Socialist and Marxist propaganda is so prevalent in textbooks that entire books have been written exposing that fact. Some textbooks coming out in recent years are so distorted, that even the very liberal group, *The People for the American Way*, came out protesting the fact that one set of new American history textbooks were completely off-base when they discussed America's founding without ever mentioning any role religion had played in early America.

To cite just one specific example about just how far all of this has gone, several pages are quoted from the book, *None Dare Call It Education*, by John Stormer:

> A textbook widely used in something called "new-new math" was the focus of a lengthy June 9, 1997 speech in the United States Senate by Democrat Senator Robert Byrd (West Virginia). He said: *Over the past decade I have been continually puzzled by our Nation's failure to produce better students despite public concern and despite the billions of Federal dollars which are appropriated annually for various programs intended to aid and improve education.* Byrd asked whether a new approach to teaching math could be why U.S. students rank 28th in the world in math. Byrd said: *Apparently the concept behind this new-new approach to math is to get kids to enjoy mathematics and hope that the "enjoyment" will lead to a better understanding of basic math concepts. Nice thought, but nice thoughts do not always get the job done.*
>
> Byrd then told of a professor at Arizona State University, Marianne Jennings. She found that even though her teenage daughter was getting an "A" in Algebra I, she could not solve a simple mathematical equation. Curious as to why, she checked her daughter's algebra book. Titled, *Secondary Math: An Integrated Approach — Focus on Algebra*, it was produced by Addison-Wesley, a major publisher of textbooks. The book has 25 authors and contributors, plus four "multicultural reviewers." Byrd commented: *Why we need multicultural reviewers of an algebra textbook is a question I would like to hear someone answer.* Byrd said the opening section entitled, "Getting Started," confirmed his suspicions about the "quirky fuzziness of this new-new approach to math." It tells the student: In the twenty-first century, computers will do a lot of the work that people used to do. Even in today's workplace, there is little need for someone to add up daily invoices or compute sales tax. Engineers and scientists already use computer programs to do calculations and solve equations.
>
> Byrd then asked and commented: *What kind of message is sent*

by that brilliant opening salvo? It seems to tell students, "Don't worry about all this math stuff too much. Computers will do all that work for us in a few years."

Byrd said, "Can you imagine such a goofy passage in a Japanese math textbook?" The "Algebra" book has "lectures" on endangered species, air pollution, and facts about the Dogon people of West Africa, chili recipes, a discussion of hot peppers and the role Zoos should play in today's society. Page 5 has its headlines written in Spanish, English and Portuguese, a map of South America showing which language is spoken where, followed by the United Nations Declaration of Human Rights in three languages. Byrd adds: *By the time we get around to defining an algebraic expression we are on page 105. But it isn't long before we get off that boring topic to an illuminating testimony by Dave Sanfilippo, a driver with United Parcel Service. Sanfilippo tells the students that he "didn't do well in high school mathematics..." but is doing well at his job now because he enters "...information on a pocket computer..."* That is hardly inspirational stuff for a kid struggling with algebra.

Byrd went on to tell the United States Senate:

By this time I was thoroughly dazed and unsure whether I was looking at a science book, a language book, a sociology book, or a geography book...The textbook tries to be all things to all students in all subjects and the result is a mush of multiculturalism, environmental and political correctness, and various disjointed discussions on a multitude of topics...This awful textbook obviously fails to do in 812 pages what Japanese textbooks do so well in 200. (That's why) the average math score in Japan is 80. In the United States it is 52.

Byrd said that having reviewed the book: *I now have a partial answer to my question about why we don't produce better students despite all the money that Federal taxpayers shell out.* Byrd concluded with this word of advice for parents: *The lesson here is for parents to follow Marianne Jennings' lead and take a close look at their children's textbooks to be sure that the new-new math and other similar nonsense has not crept into the local school system.*

That is a very clear example of how just one book (of many, many) is used to dumb-down our kids.

In 1932, William Z. Foster, a long-time Communist leader in America wrote a book that is also very revealing. The book is actually a forerunner of Skousen's book, but written from the Communist perspective. The name of the book is **Toward a Soviet America**. On page 316 of that book, Foster writes that,

> Among the elementary measures the American Soviet government will adopt to further the cultural revolution are the following; the schools and colleges and will be coordinated and grouped under the National **Department of Education** and its state and local branches. The studies will be revolutionized, being cleansed of religious, patriotic and other features of the bourgeois ideology. The students will be taught on the basis of Marxian dialectical materialism, internationalism and the general ethics of the new Socialist society. Present obsolete methods of teaching will be superseded by a scientific pedagogy.

It took the Reds 47 years to accomplish this Goal, but in 1979 under President Jimmy Carter the **Department of Education** was established. This was so clearly unconstitutional that even main-stream Republicans jumped on the bandwagon to abolish the Department. In 1996, the Republican Party made abolition of the Department a cornerstone of their campaign promises; calling it an inappropriate federal intrusion into local, state, and family affairs. The GOP platform read:

> The Federal government has no constitutional authority to be involved in school curricula or to control jobs in the market place. This is why we will abolish the Department of Education, end federal meddling in our schools, and promote family choice at all levels of learning.

Later in the 2000's under President George W. Bush, this was no longer the Republican stance, as President Bush actively used and expanded the Department during his years in office.

To summarize this Goal's progress: The leftists have gotten complete control of our public schools by putting the Federal Government radicals in charge. Most public schools are easily proven to be transmission belts for leftist propaganda. The curriculum has been so softened academically that the U.S. is now towards the bottom in every category compared to other countries and they have total control over the teachers' union.

Steve Jobs, of APPLE COMPUTER fame, is well known as an entrepreneur. What may not be so well known is that he was quite liberal in some political leanings. Therefore his statement in an interview with *Wired Magazine* in 1996 is astounding! He said, "I've come to the inevitable conclusion that the problem (in education) is not one that technology can hope to solve. No amount of technology will make a dent. It's a political problem. The problems are sociopolitical. The problems are unions. You plot the growth of the National Educational Association (NEA) and the dropping of SAT scores, and they're inversely proportional."

The bottom line is until the control of the NEA is pried away from the radicals and given back to the teachers, this system is hopeless!

It is sad to see how each detailed point Skousen made has come to pass – exactly! Yet, as mentioned, few Goals listed seemed to be so unfathomable when written! Remember, in 1958, the biggest disciplinary problem in our public schools was, "gum chewing." Now, many schools require armed guards and some students graduate who can't even read. Think about that. How have we acquiesced to such a point that as taxpayers we allow a system to continue on that graduates high school students who can't read? Did this "dumbing-down" and brainwashing happen by accident or were there forces at work that had a plan and have been working feverishly to carry it out? **No Goal has been more totally accomplished!** No Goal needs more attention!

References
In Denial, John Haynes & Harvey Klehr, 2003, Encounter Books.
Conservative History of American Left, Daniel Flynn, 2008, Crown.
One Part Classroom, David Horowitz & Jacob Laksin, 2009, Crown.

The Killing of History, Keith Windschuttle, 2000, Encounter Books.
Indoctrination, Kyle Olson, Author House, 2011.
Understanding Anti-Americanism, Paul Hollander, 2004.
None Dare Call It Education, John Stormer, 1999, Liberty Bell.
Don't Let the Kids Drink Kool-Aid, Mary Beth Hicks, 2011, Regnery.
Expelled: No Intelligence Allowed, Ben Stein, DVD Documentary, 2010.

++Watch a documentary by John Stossel, on the Fox Business Network entitled, *Stupid in America,* exposing the total breakdown of our educational system.

If any reader has a child, grandchild or friend of high school age, they need to check out the website: **summit.org. It describes a program that can inoculate high school age young people before they go off to college. It is a two-week summer training seminar that gives the kids the type of information and education that is very effective in helping them get through college with their faith and principles still intact. The young people also have a great time and meet friends they will have for life. The Summit has successfully helped tens of thousands of students over the years! [On a personal note: Both of my sons met their wives at a Summit summer session.]

CHAPTER TEN

Goal No. 19: Use student riots to foment public protests against programs or organizations which are under Communist attack.
Goal No. 34: Eliminate the House Committee on Un-American Activities.

These two Goals are related by an event that occurred only two years after Skousen's book was written. In May of 1960, Communist agitators used mostly students to try and accomplish both of these Goals. They wanted to be able to stir-up and manipulate students for their various causes and they wanted to eliminate the House Committee on Un-American Activities (HCUA).

HCUA was just another one of the many House Committees set up to specialize in a particular area. No congressman can keep track and be informed on every issue, so committees are set up to be the "experts" in a given area and present the facts to the other members as various "bills" come up for votes. There are Committees on Agriculture, Appropriation, Education, Judiciary, Veterans' Affairs, etc. HCUA was set up to monitor all of the activities occurring in America that were led by or organized by forces detrimental to America's best interest. HCUA was formed in 1938. At that time it was set up to investigate the Nazi and Ku Klux Klan activities. Later, as other threats became obvious, the investigations would include fascism and communism. The Committee and staff were set up to investigate and recommend corrective measures or laws that might be needed to better protect Americans. This would seem to be an obvious, important and necessary function. Of course, the Communists had other ideas. The last thing they wanted was to have anyone monitoring and investigating their activities.

In May of 1960 the Communists moved into high gear when they manipulated the students in Berkeley, California to riot against the HCUA which was holding hearings in the area. The riot was so shocking and frightening that a film entitled *Operation Abolition* was produced by that congressional committee to show the student manipulation going on and the Communists behind it.

Time Magazine of March 17, 1961 described the film and the situation:

> Operation Abolition is a documentary film on student demonstrations against an Un-American Activities subcommittee hearing in San Francisco last May. Much of the footage concentrates on "Black Friday," May 13, when student-provoked city police turned fire hoses on the unruly, song-chanting crowd, dragged and pushed demonstrators down the steps of city hall, arrested 68 students (mostly from the University of California, some from Stanford University, San Francisco State and the University of San Francisco) on charges of inciting a riot and resisting arrest. The House Committee subpoenaed film of the incidents from two San Francisco TV stations and turned it over to a Washington movie studio for processing. With the help of Committee Researcher Fulton Lewis III, the studio edited the film. Lewis delivered the narrative, written largely by the committee staff. Its main, heavily accented points: the "riots" were a clear example of Communist crowd tactics; the students were either Communists or "Red dupes." Pennsylvania Democrat Francis E. Walter, chairman of the House Committee on Un-American Activities, estimates that more than 10 million people have seen the film since its release last July.

In 1961 millions of people viewed the film. It was shown as a wake-up call to military units and police forces all over the country. Major companies showed it to employees. Americans were alarmed and united. Millions viewed the film and were stirred.

Today, a question can be asked: "What is the dominant political philosophy of Americans – the ones who are the activists and the involved Americans?" The change in fifty years is sad and shocking. Go online and Google the film, *Operation Abolition*. You will be discouraged to see of the 431 references listed, all are negative against the film and against the HCUA. The comments and references are slanted, distorted and many outright lies! Not one decent American has taken the time or had the interest to submit a truthful listing. The "regular" folks are all too busy going to work and taking care of their families — as the enemy works on — dedicated and focused.

In 1975, for absolutely no logical reason, Congress did disband the HCUA. Hence Communist Goal No. 34 was achieved. An interesting question is, "Would 9-11 have been averted if a functioning Committee of Congress had been monitoring subversive activities?"

On the topic of agitating young people to rebel and riot, some modern music has been designed to foment youth to rebellion, revolutionary thought and activities. Some Rock and Rap music are used by Leftists to alter thoughts and actions of young people. A classic book in this regard is *Marxist Minstrels*, by David A. Noebel. It is out of print, but still available on Amazon.com. Parents with youngsters need to be informed and aware of this subtle threat.

Reference
No Wonder We Are Losing, Robert Morris, 1958.

CHAPTER ELEVEN

Goal No. 20: Infiltrate the press. Get control of book-review assignments, editorial writing, policy-making positions.
Goal No. 21: Gain control of key positions in radio, TV, and motion pictures.

It has been thoroughly documented and openly acknowledged that the mainstream media today has a strong, unashamedly leftist bias. No one on either side argues with that fact anymore. Fox News has been castigated by the Obama Administration, apparently because it presents "both sides." Only representing the progressives' side is acceptable these days. However, this bias has been present far longer than the lesser informed conservatives believe. To show how the more informed conservatives felt, even back in 1964, one need only look to the 1964 Republican National Convention.

A typical convention delegate would usually be more active and informed than those sitting on the sidelines. Because they were more informed, the Republican delegates spontaneously and uniformly reacted at that 1964 Convention towards the media covering the event. Their reaction shocked the media and the TV viewing public. Normal professional men and women were shown shaking their fists at the cameras in frustration over the tremendously biased and vicious treatment Senator Barry Goldwater, the conservative Republican nominee had already received from most media sources prior to the convention. This Convention reaction helped wake-up others to the fact that the media did have an agenda and it was biased.

Unfortunately, it goes back even further. In the 1950's, the mainstream media's coverage of Senator Joe McCarthy indicated a maliciously anti-anti-Communist bent. The senator was viciously attacked as he single-handedly tried to warn the government and the American people of the traitors within the various government circles. At the same time, the convicted Communist agent Alger Hiss was glorified as a hero. In recent years (the 1990's) the Verona Papers, the KGB and the FBI files have been released. The Verona Papers were top secret documents that the military had obtained over the years by breaking the Soviet codes. The KGB files became available after the USSR failed and their secret "cold war" files were open to American researchers. **They all show that McCarthy's only real error was that he had dramatically underestimated the degree of Communist penetration in our government.** McCarthy spoke of dozens of agents, when we now know the number of traitors was in the hundreds. For a year or so after all of these files were released, some of the media reluctantly acknowledged the reality and the errors they had made. Even the liberal foreign press got into the soul-searching. For example the *Observer of London* in 1996 stated: **"McCarthy has gone down as one of the most reviled men in U.S. history, but historians are now facing the unpleasant truth that he was right."**

It is discouraging but quite revealing to note that after a few more years, the mainstream media slowly reverted back. Knowing that most people's memories are short, they have once again made McCarthy an evil villain and "McCarthyism" the progressive's byword. An interesting side note is the challenge made by Ann Coulter. In her book, *TREASON*, she proves beyond a shadow of a doubt that McCarthy was a hero, whom the Communists venomously hated. I believe Ms. Coulter has offered a sizable reward to anyone who can name even *one innocent person* whose life was ruined by McCarthy. Of course conventional wisdom is that he viciously destroyed the lives of hundreds of innocent people. The material on McCarthy from which Coulter got much of her information came from a landmark book (published later) by M. Stanton Evans entitled, *BLACKLISTED BY HISTORY,* a classic that covers it all!

It is therefore clear that the success of Goals 20 & 21 were well on their way to being accomplished, even as Skousen was writing his book in 1958. Many people have observed this bias in the media but don't understand why it is so prevalent. It is actually fairly simple to explain. A young person with journalistic ambitions goes off to college. As already discussed and documented (Chapter 9), the universities have long since become bastions of leftist thinking. Therefore, the only point of view that the student ever hears is from the left. Then if they get a job, almost everyone around them also has a Progressive slant. Bottom line is that many journalists don't even realize what has happened to them. They had good intensions, but never had a chance. It was the only side most had ever heard. So, on and on it goes.

References
Bias, Bernard Goldberg.
The Long March, Roger Kimbell, 2000, Encounter Books.
The Enemy at Home, Dinesh D'Souza, 2008, Broadway Books.
Red Star over Hollywood, Ronald Radosh & Allis Radosh, 2006.

Website Resources
aim.org mrc.org

Conservative Radio Talk Shows
The author does not necessarily agree with all of the ideas and statements expressed on these programs, but each offers information on important topics that are often ignored by the "mainstream" media. The following is a partial list:

Rush Limbaugh	William Bennett
Glenn Beck	Mark Levine
Sean Hannity	Laura Ingraham

CHAPTER TWELVE

Goal No. 22: Continue discrediting American culture by degrading all forms of artistic expression. An American Communist cell was told to, "Eliminate all good sculpture from parks and buildings; substitute shape-less, awkward and meaningless forms."

Goal No. 23: Control art critics and directors of art museums. "Our plan is to promote ugliness, repulsive and meaningless art."

If a reader is over sixty years of age, the total success of these Goals is probably obvious. Those fifty and under may believe that "modern art" is normal and although most don't understand it, they probably believe that is because of their own lack of artistic abilities. Hence, many would be confused by the meaning or importance of these Goals.

In recent years the issue has become far more serious than the famous television account of the art critics who were informed that the painting they selected for the top prize was created by having a dog walk around on a canvas covered with wet paint.

Many may be familiar with the sickening art exhibit displayed in 1987 entitled "Piss Christ." Note the specific wording of Goal No. 23: "Control **art critics** and **directors** of art museums." With that in mind it is important to note that the photo of a crucifix submerged in a glass of the artist's urine was not only picked to be displayed by an art museum **director**, but was the winner of the "Awards in the Visual Arts" competition by the **art critics**. And to further prove the vast headway made by those in complicity within our government; this work was funded by the National Endowment for the Arts (tax dollars at work).[1] Think this through very carefully, since we have all been conditioned over time to be more and more tolerant (dumbed-down, brainwashed, etc.) to these types of things. Our government is telling us it is OK to finance this type of blasphemy, depicting Christ in this way with government funds and displayed in a government museum, but a little third-grader is sent home from a public school because she dared bring a Christmas card to school depicting Christ in a manger. That, the authorities stated, is violating the "separation of Church and state." What do we do about these despicable contradictions? Nothing!

Lest readers believe that "art" as discussed above is an isolated and extreme example, let me list another (out of many) even more blatant. The exhibition shown in New York City at the Brooklyn Museum of Art from 2 October 1999 to 9 January 2000 was met with instant protest, centering on *The Holy Virgin Mary* by Chris Ofili. Ofili's work showed a carefully rendered black Madonna decorated with a resin-covered lump of elephant dung. The figure is also surrounded by small collaged images of female genitalia from pornographic magazines; these seemed from a distance to be the traditional cherubim.

New York Mayor Rudolph Giuliani, who had seen the work in the catalogue but not in the show, called it "sick stuff" and threatened to withdraw the annual $7 million City Hall grant from the Brooklyn Museum hosting the show, because "You don't have a right to government subsidy for desecrating somebody else's religion." Cardinal John O'Connor, the Archbishop of New York, said, "one must ask if it is an attack on religion itself," and the president of America's biggest group of Orthodox Jews, Mandell Ganchrow, called it "deeply offensive." William A. Donohue, President of the Catholic League for Religious and Civil Rights, said the work "induces revulsion." Giuliani started a lawsuit to evict the exhibit from the museum. Arnold Lehman, the museum director, filed a federal lawsuit against Giuliani for a breach of the First Amendment.² Giuliani and decency lost. The court sided with the perverts. This should tell us the importance of the people appointed to be judges.

Isn't the progress we have made in art these past fifty years wonderful?

References
The Rape of the Masters, Roger Kimbell, Encounter Books, 2005.
The Marxist Minstrels, David Noebel, Summit Press, 1975.
One Nation, Two Cultures, Gertrude Himmelfarb, Vintage, 2001.
Degenerate Moderns, Michael Jones, Ignatius Press, 1993.
Modern Art and the Death of Culture, H. R. Rookmaaker, Crossway, 1994.

Chapter Twelve Notes
1. Wikipedia.
2. Wikipedia.

CHAPTER THIRTEEN

Goal No. 24: Eliminate all laws governing obscenity by calling them "censorship" and a violation of free speech and free press.
Goal No. 25: Break down cultural standards of morality by promoting pornography and obscenity in books, magazines, motion pictures, radio and TV.

Trying to explain how completely the Goals have been accomplished can be very generational. For example, we now have a generation that has never known what Goal No. 25 is even talking about. Many of the books, magazines, motion pictures, radio and TV of their entire lives have always been saturated with obscenities. Some may have seen and enjoyed viewing the reruns of TV oldies, such as *Andy Griffin, Father Knows Best, I Love Lucy, Leave it to Beaver,* etc. But they have no idea what it was like when only programs like this were available. They could not imagine that the first Jane Russell movie entitled, *The Outlaw* (released in the 1940's) was totally banned in theaters across the country. Yet today, if one visits a Blockbuster Video Store, that movie is literally listed in the "family" or G Rated section. How could this be? Simple, Goal No. 25 has long since been accomplished. In the *Outlaw* movie there was no profanity, no nudity, nothing gory; but Jane was shown lying in a hay stack, completely covered by hay, but no clothing was visible. So the imagination of young men could run wild. Should a movie like this have been banned? That's perhaps debatable, but the point here is that there were those who pushed and pushed to continue down that slippery slope until we have the situation today, where even if the movie is rated PG, many times parents are embarrassed when they take their younger children. As far as most of the PG-13, R and NC-17 rated movies go, the point is proven. What is the purpose of all of this slide into filth? Who benefits? Why would reasonable people with children of their own be determined to push this obsession with obscenity? What good comes from any of this needless filth, foul language and the bathroom humor? Of course, no one benefits except those determined to destroy our culture. As Gramsci espoused, in America the culture and morality must be destroyed first and then the Communist "takeover" can move forward. Who else would have any motive to cause this to happen?

As far as TV is concerned, it is almost impossible for a family to sit down and watch a prime time program together. Even if the program is one of the rare "family" shows, the sexually oriented commercials usually ruin it.

The published books have followed this same course. The liberal reviewers promote the leftist books and ridicule or ignore the truthful books. In addition, the progressives have gained almost total control of librarians, and thus the books that are on the shelves. Constant battles appear in the press regularly about librarians putting obscene books in the children's section, with parents objecting to no avail.

As Tim Wildmon so cleverly and succinctly summarized, "During these past fifty years we have moved from a 'Norman Rockwell' America to a 'Hugh Hefner' America."[1] That really does summarize the situation.

References
Bias, Bernard Goldberg.
The Long March, Roger Kimbell, 2000, Encounter Books.
The Enemy at Home, Dinesh D'Souza, 2008, Broadway Books.
Red Star over Hollywood, Ronald Radosh & Allis Radosh, 2006.

** **ClearPlay** is an advanced parental control technology system that allows filtering of regular DVD movies. **ClearPlay** is a technology that allows the system to automatically and seamlessly skip over objectionable materials. It also automatically eliminates objectionable language. Check out the web site: www.clearplay.com for all of the details. An excellent, very reasonably priced tool for the whole family.

Chapter Thirteen Note

1. *Agenda: Grinding America Down*, DVD Documentary, Black Hat Films, 2010 (Comments recorded during filmed Interview). See a *trailer* of this film at: AgendaDocumentary.com.

CHAPTER FOURTEEN

Goal No. 26: Present homo-sexuality, degeneracy, and promiscuity as "normal, natural, healthy."

To contrast how promiscuity is viewed today versus 1958, one simple example tells a lot. In the 1950's, any boy found with a condom in his possession at school would immediately be expelled. Today, of course, condoms are given out in the schools and the boys and girls have classes on how to properly use them. Many schools provide free abortion clinic transportation for students without any parental notification. Those of you from a younger generation, stop and think about that contrast. Really, stop and look and think and compare. How could that much change take place in a relatively short time period? It doesn't make sense, **unless there is a driving force behind the change**. Skousen exposed that driving force fifty years ago, but few were listening and fewer were informed and fewer still were fighting the good fight to stop all of this.

The entertainment industry helped explode the sexual revolution with books, movies and TV shows. Evil men with a *Playboy* mentality helped create the women's liberation movement and many gullible women followed along. Incredibly, many naive women were deceived by these men to believe they were "liberating" themselves by offering sex to any and all men without marriage. What a bonanza this created for promiscuous men. What a sad situation for the women. They gave away a precious possession for nothing in return. Sometimes it is even worse.

Women have their "boyfriends" move into their apartments or homes. They furnish their houses at no-charge, do many household chores and then "furnish themselves" to him. When their boyfriends find greener pastures and leave them, they have nothing. But, she is liberated!! What an unbelievable hoax, and many women have bought into it. Some psychologists have said this hoax was only possible in certain cases because other insidious forces of our cultural breakdown were at work. They point out that because of the breakdown of so many families, young girls are left in a home without any father. These girls, craving to be loved by a man, are vulnerable to these advances. Other girls start to panic as they are getting older. They are out of college and are still not married. Even Christian girls fall into this trap, believing that God has forgotten them. Sadly, if the girl does get married to the wrong guy in desperation she still loses when the bum is ready to move on. The leftist have also stacked that deck against the women, by putting the "no fault" divorce laws in place which destroys women's long term security. **All this has been promoted by those liberal organizations that are supposedly guarding women's rights!**

The most intriguing facet of this Goal is the statement about presenting "homo-sexuality" as normal and natural. Reader, did you think it was a "typo" when you read the word homosexual hyphenated? These days it would seem to be a grammatical mistake; however, fifty years ago the word was so rarely seen in print that it was still considered a hyphenated word. It was something rarely discussed in public and never around children. The medical profession looked upon it as deviant behavior. Psychologists were trained to help individuals escape the homosexual lifestyle. Homosexual relations were considered a sin by **all of the world's major religions!** Pastors, rabbis and other spiritual leaders offered counseling. Fifty years later, however, some liberal clergy are now performing wedding ceremonies for gay couples. Conservative pastors are becoming increasingly fearful of violating some "civil rights" law if they even read quotes from the Bible that put homosexual behavior in a bad light. The disease rates and suicide rates are ignored. With perhaps as few as 1% of the population, how is it possible that the 99% are being driven to this new enlightenment? Did it happen by accident?

A quote from a recent newspaper article indicates this trend is accelerating. An AP dispatch from what was once considered "conservative" Montana, speaks of a new sex-ed program being projected onto the public school system, reaching down to the 5 year olds. Parents appear most worried about pieces of the plan that teach first-graders about same-gender relationships, fifth graders about various forms of intercourse and high school students about erotic art. The curriculum also teaches kindergartners terms of sexual body parts… They even teach about anxiety concerning sexual performance in high school.[1]

In the 1950's any politician in any way connected to or involved with or in any way encouraging a homosexual agenda would be instantly doomed at the polls. Again, as we have done with other Goals – fast forward to today. A prominent U.S. Senator from a major state recently remarked at a dinner speech to a homosexual gathering, "… we must not rest until we have (gay) marriage in all 50 of these United States" (Sen. Charles Schumer, D-NY).[2] Not to mention that President Obama has now come out in favor of gay marriage!.

Does this mean that most homosexuals are Marxists? No, not at all. Communists are a small minority in any demographic group. They just use people to push their agenda. Having "dupes" or "useful idiots" (as Lenin called them) do their dirty work has always been one of the most successful features of communism. **Anything that undermines the traditional family is a victory for the leftists**. The Gramsci model continues!

References
The Homosexual Revolution, David A. Noebel, Summit Press. *Libido Dominandi*, E. Michael Jones, St. Augustine Press, 1999. *Our Gay Pride President*, David A. Noebel, Summit Ministries, President's Desk, 2011.

Chapter Fourteen Notes
1. *Idaho Press-Tribune*, July 15, 2010.
2. politicalwire.com, quote of the day, October 28, 2009.

CHAPTER FIFTEEN

Goal No. 27: Infiltrate the churches and replace revealed religion with "social religion." Discredit the Bible and emphasize the need for intellectual maturity which does not need a "religious crutch."

As far as the mainline denominational churches are concerned, this Goal has been virtually accomplished and has been for many years. The large, major denominations began to move away from the established biblical teachings to the so-called "social gospel" before Skousen wrote his book. For centuries in America, even before the Pilgrims arrived, Christianity was generally taught as the unique religion. True Christianity was based on a person being saved by grace (a person trusted that Christ had done all the work on the cross and the individual had only to accept that fact)[1], whereas all other religions usually required the person to "do something." Working ones way to heaven, doing ones best, hoping the good outweighed the bad, a list of "dos" and "don'ts," etc, were consistent themes. The Marxists' "social gospel" crowd, however, didn't even include those worthwhile concepts. The leftists proclaimed that giving to the poor was the major mark of a Christian. And they didn't prescribe that act in a true biblical way. As President Obama outlined in his 2012 National Day of Prayer address, it is the government who should collect these funds in the form of taxes. Then the government is to distribute the funds – not in the "Name of Christ," but by the benevolent government.

That is now the progressives' prescribed method of helping the poor. The Biblical way is for individual Christians giving directly through their church, other charitable organizations or personally.

Because of these and many other issues, over the past number of years there grew a division among the parishioners of, "what to do?" Some decided to hang in there and fight to save the church of their forefathers, while others felt that they were "fighting" all week long at their jobs and they didn't want to spend Sundays fighting also. Since early in the 20th Century, this latter group slowly left the church they had grown up in and ended up in Independent, Fundamentalist, Evangelical or various other true Bible-believing churches. For a number of years this trend was encouraging.

In more recent years the massive, anti-Christian propaganda that is so prevalent in our schools, in the media and entertainment industry, has begun to take its toll even in the Bible-believing churches. From the 1950's through 1990, the liberal churches attendance and donations declined sharply, while the Bible-believing churches were growing rapidly. Since 1990, the trends are all down, across the board. The deceivers are winning on all fronts and Christians are losing. If this battle is new to you, I would suggest some serious research. No topic could be more important! Eternity is a long time. Because of the significance of this material, nothing short of a careful Bible study could begin to determine and understand all of the implications. The Communists have been extremely successful in this area. Goal No. 27 has basically been accomplished!

References
The Holy Bible
God versus Socialism, McDurmon, 2009 (paperback).
Total Truth, Nancy Pearcey & Phillip Johnson, Crossway, 2008.
God in the Wasteland, David Wells, Inter-Varsity Press, 1994.

**For further research, see Wikipedia – J. B. Mathews [Investigate his work in this area.]

Chapter Fifteen Note
1. Ephesians 2: 8, 9 (For by grace are you saved through faith… it is the gift of God, not of works, lest any man should boast.)

CHAPTER SIXTEEN

Goal No. 28: Eliminate prayer or any phase of religious expression in the schools on the ground that it violates the principle of "separation of church and state."

In 1962 the reinterpreting of our Constitution in this area began in full force. As briefly discussed in the **Introduction** and repeated here: our country is based upon a Christian heritage. Many may not be aware of the historical fact that for several hundred years of our country's beginnings, almost all schools and colleges in America were Christian, the Bible was a standard textbook, the Ten Commandments were posted and prayer opened each school day. A stark example of this complete turnaround is Harvard University. It is now a very liberal, secular college – actually hostile to Christianity, yet it was founded as a Christian college. Its early motto was *Veritas Christo et Ecclesiae,* "Truth for Christ and the Church." Only since 1962 have all of these biblical foundations and traditions slowly been ruled unconstitutional, **even though they were all accepted and practiced by the people** *who wrote the Constitution*! How is that possible?

It was in New York that the Supreme Court reversed hundreds of years of American traditions and almost 200 years of accepted Constitutional law. They first ruled against public school prayer in the 1962 case of *Engle v. Vitale.* The decision struck down a New York State law that required public schools to begin the school day either with Bible reading or recitation of a specially-written, nondenominational prayer.¹ (And remember, that was New York, a very liberal State!) While any other book is "fairgame" to be read and studied in the public schools, the Bible was banned in 1963.² It is fine to read books by Karl Marx extolling the wonders of communism or even books by Adolf Hitler. The Koran, the Muslim's bible, is fine. Books of violence are protected, of course, by the first Amendment. Pornographic books are deemed enlightening, but the Bible is banned. Even a Bible sitting on a teacher's desk unopened, is deemed dangerous, and not allowed.

Once the progressives realized that the Church was not going to object or protest to these decisions, the floodgates opened. The Ten Commandments, posted in American public schools for almost 400 years, were suddenly found to be unconstitutional. In 1992, it was no longer allowed to have an invocation or benediction at any public school event. In 2000, all prayers prior to sporting events were banned.³ Meanwhile, **Christians, by and large, stayed silent while all of this was being carried out.** Apparently, they had been convinced (brainwashed) that Christians should not be involved with "dirty" politics. They did not realize that their silence was actually supporting and allowing the evil advances!

> **SIDE NOTE** (Other Ivy League Schools' original mottos):
> Yale   - Light and Truth
> Princeton   - Under the Protection of God
> Columbia   - In Thy Light shall we see light
> Brown   - In God we Hope
> Dartmouth   - The voice of one crying in the wilderness

The *American Defense Fund* of Scottsdale, Arizona produced an article that summarizes the entire "separation of church and state" issue. The following is a condensed version of that article:

> To believe that the Constitution requires a total separation of church and state is to believe a lie. Nowhere in the Constitution, the Declaration of Independence, or any other founding documents of this nation will one find the phrase so often used today, "separation of

church and state." Rather, the First Amendment to the U.S. Constitution specifically provides that, "Congress shall make no law respecting an establishment of religion, or prohibiting the free exercise thereof; or abridging the freedom of speech, or of the press; or the right of the people peaceably to assemble, and to petition the government for a redress of grievances." Significantly, the phrase "separation of church and state" is not even mentioned in the Congressional Record from June 7 to September 25, 1789, the period that documents the months of discussions and debates of the 90 men who framed the First Amendment. Had separation been the intent of the First Amendment, it seems logical that the phrase would have been mentioned at least once. In fact, the phrase "a wall of separation between church and state" was not even penned until 1802, 13 years after passage of the First Amendment. In a personal, private letter to a group of Baptist pastors in Danbury, Connecticut, Thomas Jefferson (who was not one of the 90 framers) used that phrase to assure the pastors that the newly formed federal government would not establish a specific denomination of Christianity. Even so, no doubt exists that the framers of the Constitution intended that there be a differentiation between the church and the government, thus the words, "Congress shall make no law respecting an establishment of religion, or prohibiting the free exercise thereof." The church and the government were to be separate and distinct, yet both were to cooperate with each other. As evidence that our founding fathers understood the interplay of religion and government, not the separation thereof, note the following quotations:

- George Washington: *"It is impossible to rightly govern the world without God and the Bible."*
- Thomas Jefferson: *"The Bible is the cornerstone of liberty.... Students' perusal of the sacred volume will make us better citizens, better fathers, and better husbands."*
- Andrew Jackson: "That Book [the Bible] is the rock on which our Republic rests."
- Ulysses S. Grant: *"Hold fast to the Bible.... To the influence of this Book we are indebted for all the progress made in true civilization and to this we must look as our guide in the future."*

The Christian heritage of this nation, as well as the influence of the truths of Christ and His Word in our nation's government, is evidenced not only in the words of our founders, but in the government buildings themselves. For example:

- The Ten Commandments hang over the head of the chief justice of the Supreme Court.
- In the House and Senate chambers appear the words, "In God We Trust."
- On the walls of the Capitol dome appear the words, "The New Testament according to the Lord and Savior Jesus Christ."
- Engraved on the metal cap on the top of the Washington Monument are the words "Laus Deo" (Praise be to God). Also, numerous Bible verses line the walls of the stairwell.
- The Eighty-Third Congress set aside a room in the Capitol Building exclusively for the private prayer and meditation of members of Congress.

Despite the claims of many, Jefferson's "wall of separation" does not mean, and was not meant to mean, the exclusion of people of faith from impacting, participating in, or shaping government. Rather, it referred to the limit of the federal government from exercising any authority in matters of religion. The phrase "separation of church and state" was not used to the detriment of people of faith until the Supreme Court picked it up in 1947 in *Everson v. Board of Education*. But even the Supreme Court acknowledges the significant role Christianity played in the founding of our country, as well as the influence of Christian teaching on our nation. Consider the following statements from various Supreme Court opinions.

- 1892 *Church of the Holy Trinity v. United States*: "Our laws and our institutions must necessarily be based upon and embody the teachings of the Redeemer of mankind. It is impossible that it should be otherwise, and in this sense and to this extent our civilization and our institutions are emphatically Christian."
- 1952 *Zoarach v. Clauson*: "The First Amendment does not say that in every and all respects there shall be a separation of church

and state…. We find no constitutional requirement which makes it necessary for government to be hostile to religion and to throw its weight against efforts to widen the effective scope of religious influence."
- 1971 *Lemon v. Kurtzman*: "Separation is not possible in the absolute sense. Some relationship between government and religious organizations is inevitable."
- 1985 *Wallace v. Jaffree*: "The 'wall of separation between church and state' is a metaphor based on bad history, a metaphor which has proved useless as a guide to judging. It should be frankly and explicitly abandoned."

As the writer and theologian Dr. Francis Schaeffer wrote in his classic book (How Should We Then Live?) decades ago, we are now living in a "post-Christian" America. It is no doubt true that we no longer live in a Christian nation; however, there are many revisionists who try to argue that our country's founding was not based upon Biblical and Christian principles at all. That this is totally incorrect is seen by carefully rereading the United States Supreme Court decision of 1892 quoted above: "Our laws and our institutions must necessarily be based upon and embody the teachings of the Redeemer of mankind. It is impossible that it should be otherwise, and in this sense and to this extent our civilization and our institutions are emphatically Christian… [This] is a Christian nation."[4]

This was a *unanimous* decision of the Court made over 100 years after our Country's beginning! If after one hundred years our Court still determined that we were founded as a Christian nation, it logically follows that we began with that heritage, as numerous recent scholars have proven. Of all of the revisionists' writings, the most ridiculous one is claiming that we were not founded on biblical principles. The evidence otherwise is overwhelming!

References
The Soul of the American University, George Marsden, Oxford Press, 1996.

The Christian History of the Constitution, Verna M. Hall, Foundation for American Christian Education, 1983.
The Bible and the Constitution, Verna Hall and Rosalie Slater, F. A. C. E., 1983.

Website Reference
Wallbuilders.com (David Barton, President).

Chapter Sixteen Notes
1. firstamendmentcenter.org.
2. ibid.
3. ibid.
4. vftonline.org.

CHAPTER SEVENTEEN

Goal No. 29: Discredit the American Constitution by calling it inadequate, old-fashioned, out of step with modern needs, a hindrance to co-operation between nations on a worldwide basis.

Goal No. 30: Discredit the American founding fathers. Present them as selfish aristocrats who had no concern for the "common man."

The battle line of the last fifty years (and even before) was between those who interpreted the Constitution based upon the "original intent" and those who viewed it as a "living document"– which is just another way of saying that our Constitution needs to "change with the times." Ever since Franklin Roosevelt's appointments became a majority on the Supreme Court, the pendulum has swung over to the "living document" mentality. Sometimes more and sometimes less, but over those years, many conservatives believe that unconstitutional decisions (viewed from an original intent premise) have been made to change our way of life. Progressives have used this "stacked deck" to by-pass the Constitution.

The *Roe v. Wade* decision allowing women to legally abort their babies is the best known and the most controversial decision, but it is only one of many where conservative legal scholars believe that instead of trying to correctly interpret the Constitution, many judges are simply writing new laws.

Even Bob Woodward (a liberal of Watergate fame) wrote in a January 22, 1989 column in the *Washington Post* that:

> Ever since the Supreme Court issued its controversial abortion decision Roe v. Wade 16 years ago today, many legal scholars and millions of other critics have cried foul. They have argued that the court was legislating social policy and exceeding its authority as the interpreter, not the maker, of law. New evidence has now surfaced that some of the justices who wrote and supported the opinion were doing precisely that, in at least part of the decision. The opinion's author, Justice Harry A. Blackmun, said in one internal court memo that he was drawing "arbitrary" lines about the times during pregnancy when a woman could legally receive an abortion. In another memo, Justice Potter Stewart, who joined the Blackmun opinion, said the determination in the opinion about these lines was "legislative." In his dissenting opinion in *Doe v. Bolton*, Justice Byron White, joined by Justice William Rehnquist, wrote:

> > I find nothing in the language or history of the Constitution to support the Court's judgment. The Court simply fashions and announces a new constitutional right for pregnant mothers ... and, with scarcely any reason or authority for its action, invests that right with sufficient substance to override most existing state abortion statutes. The upshot is that the people and the legislatures of the 50 states are constitutionally disentitled to weigh the relative importance of the continued existence and development of the fetus, on the one hand, against a spectrum of possible impacts on the mother, on the other hand. As an exercise of raw judicial power, the Court perhaps has authority to do what it does today; but, in my view, its judgment is an improvident and extravagant exercise of the power of judicial review that the Constitution extends to this Court.

That pretty much says it all for the first part of Goal 29 which also states that our Constitution is a, "hindrance to cooperation between nations on a *worldwide* basis." Until recent years it was difficult to know what this was even talking about. It didn't seem to make any sense. Once again Mr. Skousen's incredible knowledge of the long range Communist plans proved accurate. Always keep in mind that Skousen didn't invent these Goals as a "possible way" the Communists could work; but rather, he simply wrote what he knew of their plans from his knowledge of their writings and of their activities through FBI informants.

As the courts move further and further away from interpreting the Constitution and more into the pattern of writing new laws, many critics (as seen above) are putting more and more pressure on the judges to quit being so arbitrary and to site the legal precedent for their decisions or better yet, to site the Constitution, as was always done in the past. The response to this has brought about an even more dangerous sidestep and indicates what Skousen was referring to when he talked about a "worldwide basis." **For the first time in American history, courts are now citing foreign law as precedents.**

In July 2006, Gun Owners Foundation published a paper entitled "Assessing the Threat to Second Amendment Rights Posed by the U.S. Supreme Court's Use of Foreign Law In Constitutional Interpretation."

This paper critically analyzes two recent Supreme Court cases (*Roper v. Simmons*, and *Lawrence v. Texas*) in which the Court has relied on international law to sustain constitutional challenges. In *Roper*, the Court overturned a Missouri law permitting capital punishment for 16 and 17 year olds, and in *Lawrence*, the Court overturned a Texas law prohibiting certain homosexual acts primarily because of foreign authorities. Additionally, the paper reviews the pros and cons of relying on such foreign sources in other areas. Recently, the United Nations has been pursuing a goal of eliminating all private ownership of firearms world-wide. If the Court continues to base its constitutional decisions on foreign law, the American people may find their Second Amendment right to keep and bear arms seriously undermined because of trends in countries which have had historic hostility to private firearms ownership and because of the U.N.'s penchant to restrict firearms possession and use to government officials.

Now it becomes clear that we are moving in a direction towards world law and world governance, as Goal 29 projected. Some states are now so concerned about this trend that they are offering bills to prevent state judges from citing any "foreign" precedents when deciding cases. The so-called *U.N. Agenda 21* project is a massive and comprehensive plan to be taken globally to accomplish this and much more. The program is carefully crafted and is steadily moving forward without most Americans even being aware of its existence.

As mentioned in other Chapters, it is amazing how brazen the progressives have become. They must believe there is no turning back now. Yet it is hard to imagine that United States Supreme Court Justice Ruth Bader Ginsburg could be so open as to appear on Egyptian television and state that she would not "look to the United States Constitution if I were drafting a constitution in the year 2012." Rather she suggested that the Egyptians look to the South African Constitution as much more suitable.

Goal No. 30 has been grouped with No. 29 because if the Founding Fathers are discredited, then it is much easier to move past the Constitution. Undermining our Founding Fathers has been an ongoing thrust for decades. Instead of teaching about how brave, brilliant and dedicated these men were, as accurately presented in our history books for hundreds of years, they are now often described as aristocrats, slave owners, selfish, adulterers and worse. These men who wrote in the Declaration of Independence that they were willing to give "their lives, fortunes and sacred honor to establish America" (and most of them did) are now vilified or ignored by many of our present-day historians. Ignored is an understatement. In some American history texts and reference books, more space is given to Marilyn Monroe and Elvis Presley than to George Washington!

References
Confronting the Constitution, Alan Bloom, 1992.
The Making of America, Cleon Skousen, Ensign, 1985.
Vindicating the Founders, Thomas West, 2001.
Taking the Constitution Seriously, Walter Berns, 1991.

The Five Thousand Year Leap, Cleon Skousen, Ensign, 2009.
Founding Fathers, M. E. Bradford, University Press of Kansas, 1994.
Betrayed by the Bench, John Stormer, Liberty Bell Press, 2006.

Web Addresses (Concerning the U.N. Agenda 21 Project) www.sovereignty.net, www.freedomadvocates.org

CHAPTER EIGHTEEN

Goal No. 32: Support any Socialist movement to give centralized control over any part of the culture*: education, social agencies, welfare programs, mental health clinics, etc.

This is a very significant Goal. The process of increasing the size of the federal government is fundamental to all of their socialistic plans. Notice the key words *health, education* and *welfare* mentioned in the Goal. In 1958 the Department of Health, Education and Welfare (HEW) had only been very recently established. Highly likely Skousen had written his first draft even before HEW had been started! Previously the federal government had little to do with any of those items that were handled mostly at the state level. The major purpose of the federal budget from the beginning was to fund the military to protect the citizens. Woodrow Wilson was President in the early 1900's. He was the initial instigator of increasing the size, scope and control of the federal government. Since then, only two American presidents have **ever** tried to reduce the centralized control of the federal government: Presidents Coolidge and Reagan.

---

*It is extremely impressive that Skousen used the word "culture" back in 1958. No one then was talking about our "culture" per se, and certainly not in relation to the Communist advances.

In **1958 the Federal Budget**[1] was broken down as follows. The numbers in brackets below are the inflation[2] adjusted numbers for 2010:

Health Care	$1.1 Billion	
Education	1.8	
Welfare	2.6	
Sub Total	$5.5 Billion	[$41.1]
Pensions	10.2	[$76.2]
Defense	51.8	[$387.05]
TOTAL	$86.1 Billion	[$643.34]
National Debt	$276.5 Billion	[$2,064.51]

As is seen, the total inflation adjusted Defense Department budget was over 60% of the total federal budget in 1958. This is as it should be.

By 2009, the HEW Department had been made into several separate departments (as the bureaucracy continued to expand and grow). The totals are broken down as follows:

Health Care	$764.4 Billion
Education	90.8
Welfare	406.9
Sub Total	$1,262.1 Billion
Pensions	738.6
Defense	794
TOTAL	$3,517.7 Billion
National Debt	$11.9 Trillion

Check out: **usdebtclock.org** to see the our national debt in real time. **As of January, 2012 the total is $15.3 Trillion!**

The total Defense Department budget of $794 Billion also includes all the money spent on the wars in Iraq and Afghanistan. This "war spending" does not create any new weapons systems or upgrades to protect us in the future. Notice the dramatic contrast, that by 2009 the defense budget, even including the fact we were at war, was now less than 23% of the total budget as compared to over 60% in 1958!

The total federal budget went from $643.34 Billion (inflation adjusted) in 1958 to over $3,518 Billion in 2009. Without thinking, some might erroneously conclude that the reason is simply because of our population growth. Sorry, that doesn't fly. Our population went from 173.3 million in 1958 to 307 million in 2009. That is not even doubling. Yet the budget is now almost SIX TIMES what it was then! I don't think even the most optimistic Communist would have expected such a massive takeover by the federal government in such a relatively short period of time.

Health Care

One of the giant steps forward in the total government takeover in America came when the Obamacare Bill was passed. What is equally significant about the passage of this bill is the fact that every poll showed a majority of Americans were against it and the politicians knew it. Yet it passed anyway. That is an important "first" in American political history. Why would congress do this knowing it could cost them at the next election? (And in the 2010 elections – it did, as many "Tea Party" candidates replaced the liberals.) Too many in Washington are more dedicated to the Socialist transformation of America than they are to even keeping their own jobs. Some cynics would say that they really didn't have to worry about their jobs as they were promised even more lucrative payoffs if they voted right. The cynics were correct.

Obama had a Democrat super-majority in the House and Senate. This bill was never seen in advance by the Republicans and no real debate was allowed. In an unprecedented event, it passed without a single Republican vote in the House or Senate. Remember the Speaker of the House, Nancy Pelosi, telling the congress that we have to, "pass this bill to find out what is in it." Unbelievable!

USA TODAY summarized the economic scope of the health care industry in America [6/21/09]:

Q: How big a part of the economy is health care?
A: It accounts for about one-sixth of the entire economy — more than any other industry. Spending on health care totals about $2.5 trillion, **17.5%** of our gross domestic product (a measure of the value of all goods and services produced in the United States). That's up from 13.8% of GDP in 2000 and **5.2% in 1960,** when health spending totaled just $27.5 billion — **barely 1% of today's level,** according to the Kaiser Family Foundation, a nonpartisan health policy group.[3] Those numbers are for total health care spending (individual, companies and government). More frightening is to see the astronomical growth in the federal portion of this spending during the same time period.

Figure 3 below is a graph showing just the government health care spending. The actual figures are shown from 1958 to 2009. With estimated figures from 2009 to 2015. The graph is bad enough, but many qualified observers feel that the cost of Obamacare is **drastically** being underestimated, as government entitlement programs are when they begin.

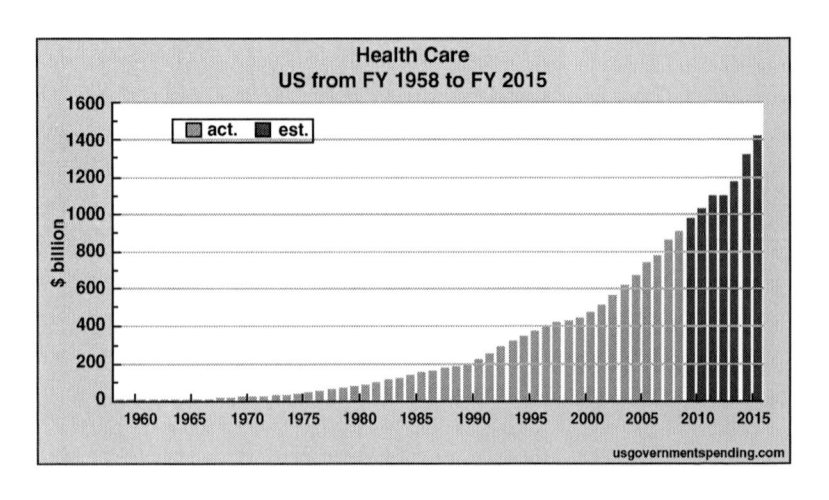

Health Care Spending (1958 – 2015)
Figure 3

The Great Society

In addition to the huge financial tax burden that all of this welfare spending created, there was a much more tragic downside – the human loss. One welfare bill created by the "Great Society" programs under Lyndon Johnson has nearly destroyed the black family. The Aid to Families with Dependent Children (AFDC) program was originally created to help widows with children. Even the original program was a misguided government intrusion, as for centuries in America, church groups, family members or the local community had done a great job caring for their own. With the Great Society, the program was disastrously expanded to include aid to any woman with children, as long as there was no male in the household. At first thought this might sound somewhat reasonable. A woman with young children at home can't work, so she and the kids will all starve? The theory was with the AFDC check coming in, they could get by. Of course, the more children, the larger the government check. Remember, if there are any adult males in the home, married or not, the checks stop immediately. Therefore, the message to the young women is to have as many illegitimate children as possible, and make absolutely sure you do not get married to the father! Not only a horrible situation, but think of all of the young children being raised without a father, or the young males with no role model at all. Is it any wonder that many young boys gravitate to gangs and crime. A number of black leaders have very belatedly spoken out against these programs in recent years (Bill Cosby for one), as it is obviously destroying many families. [Also note how this law works to help accomplish Goals 40 and 41, as discussed in Chapter 23.]

A few politicians did understand that there was a better way. President Reagan, long vilified by black leadership, had an amazing record for improving black economic achievements. As black radio commentator Larry Elder summarized, the Reagan "tax cuts for the rich" and his "trickle down" economic theories cut black unemployment from 20% (under Carter) down to 11% by 1989. (Compare that 11% to the present rate of black unemployment under President Obama, which is 16.7%).[4] Also under Reagan, black-owned businesses grew by 38%, three times the rate of all other businesses, which themselves were all growing at astounding rates. As black Rep. Allen West (R.-FL) recently said, "For far too long the choice has been to give a handout instead of a hand up. Our liberal politicians continue the same old tired policies of dependence on big government." Two books have recently been written to show the overwhelming evidence pertaining to which political party has been the one fighting for true civil rights. The facts are totally contrary to what most minority people believe today. [*Stolen History*, by Franz Kebreau and *Demonic*, by Ann Coulter]. As both of those books document, **every politician who has ever fought against any civil rights legislation has been a Democrat!**

Now history is repeating itself. Not satisfied with destroying black families, the Democrats are going after all families of all races. When the Obama pollsters discovered that 70% of unmarried women voted for Obama, they realized this was a "gold mine" for a new voting bloc to be exploited. By making many black people dependent upon government, they had "purchased" a 90% voting bloc (i.e.; 90% of blacks vote for the liberals, to keep the checks rolling in). In order to capitalize on this new bloc and to also expand it, Obama incorporated into the Health Care Bill (of all places) a section that rewards with tax advantages women who cohabitate, but do not marry. One reason we are losing the battle is that it is hard for moral Americans to realize just how evil the opposition really is.

Environmental Movement

A major new area has come on the scene since 1958 that allows the government centralized control over everything. This is one sphere that even the Communists could never have imagined, yet it has become **their most powerful weapon!** There was no environmental movement or organization back in the 1950's. As the public became aware of the developing water and air pollution problems, increasingly more citizens became concerned. Environmental groups organized to encourage better management of our ecosystem. While there were some extremists groups from the beginning, many of the original leaders had serious questions and provided worthwhile leadership. A number of necessary laws were passed to stop the pollution. By the 1980's most all of the needed corrections had been made and the results were beneficial and obvious. From cleaner air to sparkling water, Americans had "wised up." Unfortunately, the Communists began to realize the potential of this issue to completely collapse capitalism through regulations. The co-founder of Greenpeace (one of the original environmental groups) said recently on a video interview, that the environmental movement has been high-jacked by the Reds. Patrick Moore flatly stated *"**Environmental extremism emerged because world communism failed, the wall came down and a lot of peaceniks and political activists moved into the environmental movement, bringing their neo-Marxism with them. They learned to use 'green language' in a clever way to cloak agendas that actually have more to do with anti-capitalism than with ecology or science.⁵"**

It is very revealing how little real concern the Red environmentalists have. They work day and night to halt an industry in America. When they have succeeded, the necessary product is then imported from China. Of course the pollution produced in unregulated China to make this same product is many times that caused by the much more efficient American counterpart.

The Communists and their Progressive collaborators initiated the idea of "global warming" as a way to tax and regulate capitalism out of existence. In 2009 I wrote a Letter-to-the-Editor that briefly summarized the total stupidity of this whole idea and tried to explain why these concepts "grow legs" in the academic community and then on through the media:

---

*Moore's statement has the most far-reaching implications of any paragraph in this book. While many other factors and forces are at work to destroy our country, the environmental extremists now in charge of our Environmental Protection Agency can alone do the job! Using the innocent sounding "green agenda" they have no opposition. Through the public schools, our kids have been totally brain washed on this and related subjects. Have you ever thought about the fact that millions of children have been legally murdered in their mother's womb, but if someone destroys the eggs of an eagle, it's literally a prison sentence!

October 4, 2009
Dear Editor,
The ignorance parroted in the media concerning *Global Warming* is almost unprecedented. I happen to have a Doctor of Science degree from Washington University, although that is not at all required to see through this farce. However, having taught at three major universities did give me the background to understand how all this misinformation could continue. Professors must "publish or perish." Therefore, they will write proposals based upon what the "in-crowd" wants to hear. So, if the government propagandists are pushing global warming for their own political reasons, then of course all of the professors will be singing the same tune, as they laugh behind their backs. I saw all of this first-hand just thirty years ago, when TIME, Newsweek and most of the media were pushing *Global Cooling*. Cover stories exclaiming that we were entering the next ice age were common. So at that time, all of the Profs' proposals were written to verify this cooling trend. Amazing — and that was just 30 years ago!

The facts are from 800 to about 1200 the world experienced the so-called *Medieval Warm Period* (they were farming in Greenland). From about 1560 until 1850, we were in the *Little Ice Age* (they were ice skating on the Thames River in London). The earth's climate has always varied (fortunately not by very much), probably controlled by sun-spot activity, having nothing whatsoever to do with the amount of carbon generated by humans! As even the New York Times admitted this past week, the warming trend has flattened out. Looks like another cooling trend is on the way. Al Gore will have to slightly revise his movie. Maybe his new, *The Coming Ice Age* film could win him another Nobel Prize.
Jim Bowers

The St. Petersburg Times (my hometown's, very liberal newspaper) did not print my letter because it was "politically incorrect." Fortunately, months after I wrote my letter the emails between various scientists promoting the global warming farce were published by a "hacker." The emails proved that the whole scheme was a fraud from the beginning. Later, even more damaging information became available as the BBC of England published an interview with one of the leading global warming proponents. The Obama Administration is ignoring all of this new information that proves that the science is not there, but worse, was **purposely falsified**. The effect of the so-called, "cap and trade" bills still floating around congress are of such significant financial magnitude that they overshadow everything else being discussed, from an economic point of view. These bills, simply put, would destroy America as we know it! Therefore all citizens should understand and be vigilant on this topic. An article that very succinctly summarizes this fraud was written by Dr. E. Calvin Beisner and published in the Schwarz Report Newsletter of April 2010:

> Forget all you've heard about unprecedented global warming; global warming so rapid it can't be natural, but must be anthropogenic; global warming threatening to devastate economies, ecosystems and perhaps even human civilization itself global warming on which "the science is settled" and "the debate is over." Forget it all!
>
> Last Saturday (February 13), Dr. Phil Jones, the onetime director of Climate Research Unit at the University of East Anglia (until he stepped down in December under investigation for scientific misconduct) and the provider of much of the most important data on which the U.N. Intergovernmental Panel on Climate Change (IPCC) and many governments have based fears of unprecedented global warming starting in the mid-1970s, gave an interview to the BBC in which he made some shocking revelations. Keep in mind, as you read the list of the revelations below, that the BBC has been a major proponent of belief in dangerous anthropogenic global warming (DAGW) and indeed has billions of dollars of its pension funds invested in ventures that stand to benefit from that belief. Its interviewer was by no means hostile to Jones, did not follow up when Jones's answers were less than forthcoming, and generally simply gave Jones a platform from which to attempt to vindicate himself and the theory he has long promoted. Nonetheless, in the interview Jones:
>
> 1. Admitted that he did not believe that "the debate on climate change is over" and that he didn't "believe the vast majority of

climate scientists think this" (Al Gore, Barack Obama, Barbara Boxer, did you hear that? Greenpeace, World Wildlife Fund, Sierra Club, Friends of the Earth, Union of Concerned Scientists, did you hear that? Ed Begley, Robert Kennedy, Richard Cizik, Jim Ball, did you hear that?).

2. Admitted that there was no statistically significant difference between rates of warming from 1860-1880 and 1910-1940 and the rate from 1975-1998, though he and other DAGW believers had for years said the rate in the last period was unprecedented and therefore couldn't be natural but must be manmade.
3. Admitted that there has been no statistically significant warming for the last 15 years (though he personally believes this is only a temporary pause in manmade warming).
4. Admitted that natural influences could have contributed to the 1975-1998 warming (significantly mentioning only the sun and volcanoes – the latter a brief cooling factor – completely omitting reference to ocean circulations such as the Pacific Decadal Oscillation, The North Atlantic Oscillation, and the Atlantic Multi-decadal Oscillation, and changes in cloudiness stemming from both the ocean circulations and changes in influx of cosmic rays, all of which have demonstrated to have strong effect on global temperature).
5. Admitted that the revelation of data handling failures at CRU and elsewhere (e.g., the U.K. Meteorological Office) had shaken the trust many people have in science.
6. Admitted that the Medieval Warm Period might well have been as warm as the Current Warm Period (1975-present), or warmer, and that if it was "then obviously the last 20th century warmth would not be unprecedented" (though he persisted in doubting the MWP to have been global and as warm as the present).
7. Dodged a question about a change of rules at the IPSS allowing lead authors to cite scientific papers not published by deadline, despite the Climategate emails record having shown that he was actively involved in precisely that change.
8. Said that his "life has been awful" since Climategate broke in November.

9. Dodged a question about why he had asked a colleague to delete emails relating to the IPCC's Fourth Assessment Report, asked the colleague to ask others to do likewise, and said he had already done so himself.
10. Dodged a question about whether some of his handling of data had crossed the line of acceptable scientific practice.
11. Dodged a question about the significance his writing in an email that he had used a "trick" to "hide the decline" in tree-ring temperature date.

As a former journalist, having conducted many interviews, and now often interviewed myself by journalists and talk show hosts, I can't avoid the strong impression that Jones was given the questions, or at least some, in advance and probably made lack of tough follow-up questions a condition of submitting to be interviewed. (By the way, I have never either required or granted such conditions.) His obviously having been prepared with a statistical table to refer to in answer to the first question is one of the evidences of that.

The media and government officials are belatedly opening their eyes to the deceit behind much of the global warming propaganda, as illustrated by a recent story in the St. Petersburg Times (July 29, 2011) headlined: **Global warming scientist under fire.** This was the scientist whose observations that several polar bears had drowned in the Arctic Ocean helped galvanize the movement. Now he has been put on leave and facing accusations of scientific misconduct. Of course when the issue dies down, he will quietly be reinstated.

Many people are beginning to realize that all of this global warming and *Cap and Trade* legislation are simply excuses for the government to tax us and control us even more. **Obama openly acknowledged that, "Under my plan of a cap and trade system, electricity rates would necessarily skyrocket."**[6] Ironically, candidate Obama said over and over again that there would be no new taxes on the middle class.

In all of this discussion about the economic impact of these disastrous policies, few bring up the tragic human cost. The progressives claim to always be the ones helping the poor against the evil and rich conservatives. In reality, they seem often to only care about their political goals. As just one horrific example of the effect that environmental extremism has had on innocent humans, consider the global ban these zealots initiated on eliminating the use of DDT. That one action alone has resulted in the deaths of 100 million children, mainly black under the age of five, due to malaria's return.[7]

The bottom line is that there is no energy shortage in America. We are giving foreign governments almost half of a TRILLION dollars of our own money per year just for oil imports — needlessly. This is probably the least understood and best keep secret in American. As recently reported in HeatingOil.com (February 17, 2010):

> On Monday, a report released by a national contractor for state utilities claimed that the United States contains more than 2,000 trillion cubic feet (tcf) of natural gas and 229 billion barrels (bbl) of oil. As observed by The Energy Source blog at Forbes.com, that's more than the average OPEC nation holds. Noting that a chunk of these reserves lie in areas barred from drilling, the report also found that leaving these reserves untouched would cost the US $2.36 trillion in lost GDP over the next twenty years. It's no secret that the US contains its own oil and gas reserves. According to Reuters, previous estimates have placed those figures at 1750 tcf and 186 bbl for gas and oil, respectively.
>
> The study, two years in the making, was sponsored by the National Association for Regulatory Commissioners in conjunction with the industry-funded Gas Technology Institute. The government-protected reserves amount to 43 billion barrels of oil and 286 tcf of gas and are located in the Arctic National Wildlife Refuge and in areas just off the coastline of the continental US. The US currently consumes an average of 20 million barrels of oil per day, and produces 6 million barrels per day. The research was done according to standard methodology by SAIC Corp in data collection and processing, and the report attributes the reserve increases to advances in drilling technology and gas extraction methods. The real thrust of the study comes from its economic figures. This

appears to be the first time a hard dollar amount—and a whopping one at that—has been attached to the value of those reserves.

Three Continuing Misconceptions

Before ending this Chapter which includes, "supporting any Socialist movement ….," there are three misconceptions in this general area that are almost uniformly misunderstood by both conservatives and liberals. Actually, they are not really "misunderstood," they are just wrong. Many people have been extensively brainwashed in these three key areas.

Misconception One concerns the widely accepted idea that communism and socialism are on the far left and fascism (Nazism) is on the far right of the political spectrum. Nothing could be further from the truth. This misconception came from an historical happening, not a misinterpretation of the political scene. Briefly summarized, it all began in August, 1939 when Hitler's Germany and Stalin's Soviet Union made their famous non-aggression pact, but behind the scenes they were secretly agreeing about how they were going to divide up a conquered Europe between them. They then proceeded to move in and take conquest of those countries. During this period the media reported that these two Socialist countries were on the move. The Union of Soviet *Socialist* Republics (USSR) and the National *Socialist* Party (Nazi) of Germany were now allies in this aggression against the helpless smaller countries, prior to WWII. Communist publications and Red mouthpieces, both here in the U.S. and around the world rejoiced at these wonderful events and had nothing but praise for Nazi Germany and the Pact. That two Socialist nations would unite is not surprising, as they held basically the same worldview. That they would be so openly aggressive towards their neighbors was the news. All this changed in June, 1941 when Hitler suddenly turned on Stalin and began an invasion of Russia. Instantly, all of the Communists and sympathizers turned on Germany, as would be expected. But what came out of Hitler's "move" changed the political vernacular forever. Since the Nazis were now "the enemy," all of the Communist media blasted the Fascist, as the enemies of communism.

Since communism is accepted as on the "left," anyone opposing communism must be on the "right." That was it!

A realistic and consistent view of the political spectrum is shown in Figure 4. It should seem obvious and no doubt would be, except the Communists never got over the Hitler betrayal and hence, forevermore, anyone opposed to communism or even Progressive thinking is a Fascist! No logical political reasoning, just a reaction.

Total Government Control   USA   No Government

←----------------------------------+----------------------------------

Totalitarian   Progressive   Liberal   Moderate   Conservative   Libertarian   **Anarchy**
Communism
Fascism
Socialism

Government Spectrum
Figure 4

As Figure 4 illustrates, the graph moves from right to left. The far right is represented as no government and as one moves further left it represents more and more government control, until it is 100%. The far right is clearly not fascism, but anarchy; that is, having no formal government at all. The far left includes all of those "isms" where the government has much control, such as fascism, communism and socialism – all of the totalitarian forms of government. Within these groups there are some varying degrees, of course. Some would argue that communism is much more brutal than is practiced by the so-called Socialistic countries. That is historically correct, but this is a Figure that is representing a political spectrum, not a way of life. Note that in between these two extremes fall other popular terms for political philosophies, each placed according to the approximate degree of government control. The "USA" is shown approximately where it might be seen up to about 1950. While the American people were still heavily in the conservative camp, the government was already moving rapidly to the left. The only real point here is to illustrate how ridiculous it is that in almost all media descriptions and even in textbooks, the "far right" is regularly characterized as being Fascist. Ridiculous!

Misconception Two consists of an equally incorrect, but widely held view that the way to balance the federal budget is to raise taxes – which would bring in more money. Many conservatives would erroneously agree, but would then add that spending should also be cut. The basic premise in incorrect, and has proven to be wrong in practice a number of times. In a country that is heavily taxed, increasing taxes actually reduces the funds coming into the Treasury, but reducing taxes, increases the revenue. It does seem backwards, but is better understood by viewing Figure 5, often referred to as the "Laffer Curve." Professor Arthur Laffer explained this economic concept to those in the Reagan administration who were trying to stop President Reagan from dramatically reducing taxes across-the-board.

As seen in Figure 5, if the income tax rate is zero, obviously no money comes in to the Treasury. Not so obvious, without a little thought, is the idea that if the tax rate is 100%, also no money would come in. Think about it. If the income tax rate is 100% of every penny earned, who would work? People would no doubt use the "black market" to survive, but NO ONE would want to openly earn a dime! It therefore logically follows that there is a tax rate lower than 100% that produces the maximum revenue. The exact point for maximum revenue varies depending upon the situation. For example, in the middle of WWII people would be willing to work harder for less income because of their patriotism. The point is that a way to increase government revenue and help balance the budget in a country that is already overtaxed is to reduce taxes for everyone, across-the-board. This concept has more subtle and additional benefits that cannot be accurately forecast. For example, when lowering taxes, individuals have more spending power and therefore purchase more things. This increases business and the benefiting companies hire more people. Some of these new hires may have been unemployed, so now they are also paying taxes, whereas before they weren't. Bottom line is, when a country is overtaxed, revenues greatly increase **by lowering taxes, not**

111

THE NAKED TRUTH

raising them. Of course, slashing wasteful government spending is also necessary to complete the balance. Look up the actual facts, if still unconvinced. Presidents Coolidge, Kennedy (carried out by Johnson), Reagan and (George W.) Bush all significantly cut taxes during the past one hundred years. As a result, the federal revenue increased dramatically each and every time. Unfortunately, only under Coolidge did the Congress also cut the spending. Reagan tried, but the Democrat controlled congress pushed on.

In Figure 5, assume point A is the present tax rate. By lowering the rate to point B, the revenue increases by X amount. Point C is the optimum rate, but is not a fixed value and cannot be calculated accurately as an exact science. Note that if the rate were lowered to that indicated by point D (much lower than the rate shown by point B) the revenue to the Treasury would be the same as it was for our hypothetical point B. Wouldn't it be nice if the government, for once, erred on the side of a rate too small instead

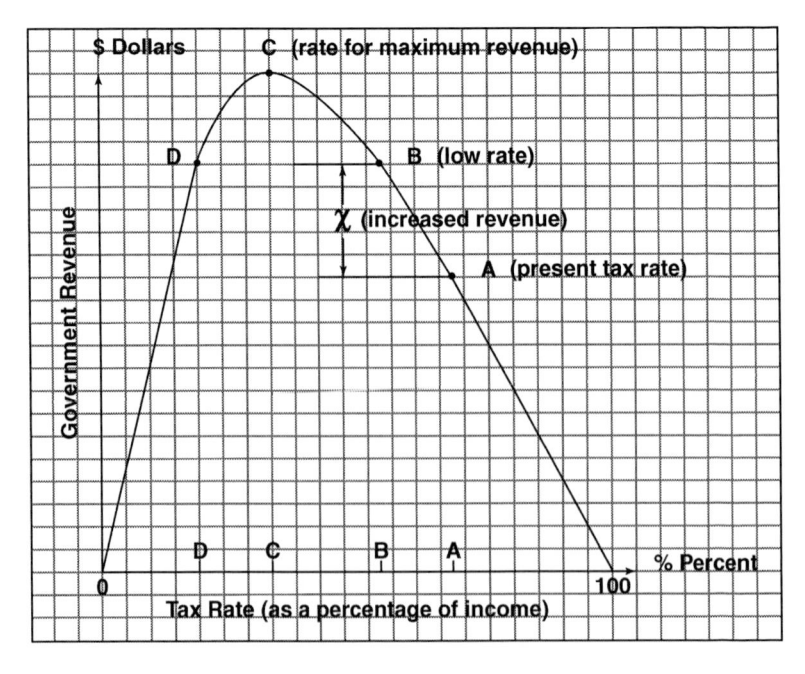

Laffer Curve [8]
Figure 5

of one too large, to obtain the same revenue? For those readers not mathematically inclined, don't try and make the interpretation of Figure 5 complicated. It is just illustrating in "picture" form that as the tax rate is reduced from 100%, the money coming into the Treasury increases and finally reaches a maximum amount as illustrated by point C. Therefore, lowering taxes (when already overtaxed) **increases** income to the government.

Misconception Three concerns the widespread belief that President Franklin Delano Roosevelt's New Deal spending spree got America out of the Great Depression. Regularly, so-called experts are touting the New Deal approach as what President Obama needs to do. Even after the nearly trillion dollar stimulus package made matters worse, not better, many of the so-called experts said it was because it wasn't enough, the government needed to spend more. The fact that government spending has never and can never bring a country out of a recession just confuses the liberal, Keynesian mind. John Maynard Keynes' theory of spending our way out of a recession has never worked, but is still being taught to the economic majors at our most prestigious colleges. What is strange is that few bother to look at the actual facts which are readily available. With continuous, massive deficit spending during the New Deal, the unemployment rate was still 14.6% in 1940. As today, many economists believe the rate was much higher; people just gave up trying to find work. Regardless, other than acquiring a huge debt, the New Deal did little to help the economy, just as Obama's spending has done little except add to the debt! **The best proof and summary of this fact actually came from FDR's own Secretary of the Treasury. In May of 1939, Secretary Henry Morgenthau bluntly acknowledged that, "We have tried spending money. We are spending more than we have ever spent before and it does not work." He concluded, "I say after eight years of this administration we have just as much unemployment as when we started … And an enormous debt to boot!"**[9] Those brainwashed by years of conventional wisdom may need to re-read that very revealing quote!

In the 1930's some people did see through this folly. Carefully study Figure 6. Note all of the small comments the artist sprinkled around this editorial cartoon from the Chicago Tribune. One can see it is really déjà vu. Exactly what informed people are worrying about today, is exactly what some were fearing back then – and rightfully so. In contrast, it seems the obvious is totally oblivious to progressives; Presidents Coolidge and Reagan took office in similarly bad times. In total contrast, they cut taxes and cut regulations and cut the spending rates (except in Reagan's case he increased military spending for our national survival). The result was the Roaring 20's of Coolidge and the longest economic boom in our history started by Reagan. To the minds of the leftists, facts never seem to matter, only their Marxists theories.

1934 Chicago Tribune Editorial Cartoon
Figure 6

Summary

Goal #32 discussed in this Chapter is the heart of America's potential downfall. All of the Goals are bad. For example, by accomplishing the first four Goals covered in Chapter One, dozens of Countries were pushed into the horrors of the Red Orbit, putting millions of people into slavery or death. **However, accomplishing Goal #32 of turning America into a Socialist State is the final step,** and this process is very difficult to reverse! A variety of facts and details have been discussed in this Chapter. Many more important facts are detailed in the reference books listed. For an easy, visual summary of how close this Goal is to completion, take a look below at the cover of Newsweek for February 16, 2009:

An award winning, comprehensive DVD video summarizes all of this material. To view the trailer, go to: **AgendaDocumentary.com** (Already viewed by over a million people.)

References
Understanding the Times, David Noebel, Summit Press, 2008.
  The Long March, Roger Kimball, Encounter Books, 2001.
  Road to Sefdom, F. Heyak, UC Press.
Soft Despotism, Paul Rahe, 2010.
The Great Global Warming Swindle (DVD), Durkin, WAGtv Production (England). [**A must-see documentary**].

Chapter Eighteen Notes
1. usgovernmentspending.com.
2. inflationdata.com.
3. kff.org.
4. money.cnn.com, September 2, 2011.
5. *The Great Global Warming Swindle*/DVD, Durkin, WAGTV Productions.
6. youtube.com, Obama, (under my plan).
7. discoverthenetworks.org.
8. heritage.org/laffer.
9. *Human Events,* Page 25, August 29, 2011.

CHAPTER NINETEEN

Goal No. 35: Discredit and eventually dismantle the FBI.

It appears that this Goal has been altered. At the time the Communist groups were planning all of these goals, J. Edgar Hoover was the Director of the **FBI**, and had been for years. Since the integrity and effectiveness of the FBI was so well established and accepted, the Communists may have decided later that it would be better in the long run to slowly infiltrate the FBI and take it over, rather than pursuing the almost hopeless task of discrediting it. They may have also realized how effective a tool it could be for them if they had control of the FBI and could use it for their purposes, like the Gestapo in Germany or the KGB in Russia. In any event, so far they have not been able to accomplish this Goal. Of all of the federal agencies, the FBI seems to have been the least influenced by left-wing individuals moving in and changing basic policies. However, some astute observers are worried about recent trends. Various appointed directors have been far more liberal than Hoover. Obviously, over time things can change, as more and more new people are hired. That fear seems to be unfolding in early 2012. Several startling developments have recently occured which would indicate that the once great and independent FBI, may have become just another government agency, doing the partisan bidding of those in power.

Another thing the Reds have accomplished, to a large degree, is to have destroyed the reputation of their arch-enemy, J. Edgar

Hoover. He was so important in setting up the FBI's modus operandi (which led to its great success) that the FBI headquarters building in Washington, D.C. is named in his honor. Yet, after he died and could not defend himself, the liberal media went all out to destroy his reputation. Unfortunately, they were quite successful. The charges made against Hoover were so preposterous that conservatives didn't even bother to speak up. When it became apparent that the wild accusations were actually "sticking," it was too late. The gullible public had accepted the charges as fact, since no counter view had been expressed. Ask the average Joe on the streets today about this great patriot and if they have an opinion at all, they will probably giggle and ask, "Isn't that the gay FBI guy who dressed up in women's clothing and went to D.C. parties?" Is it any wonder the conservatives didn't address these wild tales when they first started appearing in print? The head of the FBI, hated by most media progressives, crooks and traitors, knowing that they would be looking for any way to discredit him, would be so stupid that he would openly show up at Washington parties in drag? Not only not credible, but impossible; yet, it is now widely accepted! As Hilter taught us, a lie repeated often enough, becomes conventional truth!

SIDE NOTE: One should never underestimate just how vitriolic and persistent the leftists are. I assumed they had already smeared Mr. Hoover enough and were going to let him rest in peace. No way! As this book is going to press I note that a new movie is coming out entitled, *J. Edgar*. I can only imagine how distorted this bio will be. I hope I am proven wrong, but don't count on it. Hoover was their biggest obstacle in the early days. His classic book, *Masters of Deceit*, completely exposed them. The Commies don't forgive or forget. Poor Richard Nixon tried to get back into the good graces with the liberal crowd in his later days as President by opening the doors to Communist China. The Chinese Reds now manufacture just about everything we buy. Nixon went further and sold us out in the area of economic policies by declaring that , "We are all Keynesians now" (Time Magazine, 12/31/65). Unfortunately for him, nothing he could do would ever get him back in their favor. Why? Because he had committed the unpardonable sin of being a leader, as a young Congressman, in exposing Alger Hiss as a Communist spy. Hiss was the liberal's darling, regardless of his traitorous activities. Finally, the leftists were able to get "pay back" by forcing Nixon's resignation for the Watergate incident. That is a story in itself. What is now considered a major scandal, was nothing more than a minor break-in to an office complex by several overzealous political hacks. Probably more than a hundred more serious crimes were committed in Washington, D.C. that same night. Yet the progressives and their media allies turned this petty crime into an impeachable offense. Finally, when Nixon resigned in disgrace, the Marxists had extracted their revenge!

CHAPTER TWENTY

Goal No. 36: Infiltrate and gain control of more unions.

The conflict between communism and freedom is the problem of our time. It overshadows all other problems. ... On the outcome of this conflict depends the future of all mankind.
George Meany
President, AFL-CIO
1955

Most union workers are patriotic, with many being war veterans, but the Communists were making inroads towards one of their main Goals, many years ago. The drastic contrast between George Meany, quoted above, and the type of union official destroying our country is illustrated by an excerpt from the book *None Dare Call It Treason: Twenty-five Years Later* (John Stormer, 1992 – paperback edition) which summarizes the stance of a "different" union leader early on:

> Harry Bridges, the Australian-born Communist leader of the International Longshoremen's and Warehousemen's Union, has successfully fought government attempts to deport him and strip him of his power. With a word, Bridges can tie up all shipping of defense supplies, military equipment, etc. through the West Coast ports. His Communist associates in Hawaii have a virtual political

and economic stranglehold on our 49th State. Bridges' union was expelled from the CIO in 1950 as Communist dominated.

It is interesting to note that from all of the newsmakers and union leaders, TIME magazine chose a smiling, hard-working Harry Bridges to put on the cover of their July 19, 1937 issue. The people at TIME magazine making that choice were no doubt the same ones who just two years later hired Whittaker Chambers as an editor. At the time of his hire, Mr. Chambers was a Communist. Fortunately for America, Chambers later renounced communism and became a key player in exposing Alger Hiss as a Communist, while the Communist Harry Bridges continued to hold America hostage.

Most informed sources understood that Harry Bridges was a Communist as far back as the 1940's. The few remaining doubters were eliminated in the 1990's when the Soviet files were opened after the Berlin Wall fell. In those documents we found that Bridges was not just a Communist sympathizer, but was also on the Central Committee of the Communist Party in America, working diligently to help the Soviet Union destroy America and take over the world!

Please carefully read the following quote and realize that it was made after all of the above information was well known by all informed people. Also, to help you realize the gravity of the present situation in America, please note that the quote below was given by a person who is a powerful figure in Washington.

On July 27, 2001, Nancy Pelosi said, "Harry Bridges was arguably the most significant labor leader of the 20th Century... Beloved by the workers of this nation and recognized as one of the most important labor leaders in the world."[1] How could anyone in her position in Congress make such a statement? Worse, she has never had to answer for it and never held accountable for making it. Apparently, few know and fewer care.

In more recent times, unions such as the Service Employees International Union (SEIU) have had tremendous power in presidential politics. It is usual for unions to get involved in politics, but the question raised in this book is what kind of "worldview" do those leaders have that are now so prominent? Michelle Malkin's book, *Culture of Corruption,* has an entire chapter dealing with just the SEIU union. Malkin shows how President Obama is totally tied into SEIU, but more important to our analysis is that she shows how radical the leaders of SEIU are. Also, Glenn Beck* went into great detail on his FOX NEWS TV program concerning how much regular access and control the SEIU leaders have with the President. He has documented extensively how wildly leftist they are!

The power the unions exert in politics is extensive. When the giant automakers General Motors and Chrysler were in financial trouble because of unsustainable retirement deals they had made with their unions, they were not allowed to fail. Normally a company would declare bankruptcy and reorganize. During this process the union contracts would be put on a sound, business-viable basis. Instead, President Obama simply had the government pay out the differences, buy stock and give "loans" to ensure the union supporters would not have to share in the belttightening that everyone else has to go through in a recession. All of the union deals and pensions would simply be covered by the taxpayers. As clearly shown by Malkin and Beck, certain union leaders are no longer just pro-democrat, no longer just pro-liberal, but astonishingly, they are radical leftists – just as Skousen warned! Has this just happened by accident?

Americans are finally awakening to some of these inroads by union henchmen at the local level. The recent award winning documentary, *Waiting for Superman,* (Available from Amazon.com on DVD). shows how the entrenched teacher union bosses are destroying our education system. They are also destroying the teachers they are supposed to be representing.

---

*Glenn Beck is no longer on FOXNEWS, but has a regular program on GBTV.com

References
None Dare Call It Treason: Twenty-five Years Later (John Stormer, 1992 – paperback edition)
Culture of Corruption, Michelle Malkin, 2010
Waiting for Superman, DVD, Davis Guggenheim, Director, 2010.

Chapter Twenty Note
1. American Thinker, July 31, 2010

CHAPTER TWENTY-ONE

Goal No. 37: Infiltrate and gain control of big business.

The Marxists have not had to secretly infiltrate big business in recent times, the way they infiltrated government and universities in the 1930's. With most all of our colleges graduating brainwashed progressives or worse, many businesses are now being run by people who have no idea of how the free-enterprise system works and certainly no understanding of why it has proven to be far superior for everyone and significantly better than all of the "isms" they've been taught in college.

The strange paradox today is that the average citizen still believes the general statement that Republicans represent the party of business and Democrats are the party of labor. There is some truth in the root of this thought, but it has long since been displaced. Early on most Republicans were the champions of free-enterprise and capitalism, while most Democrats (at least from Woodrow Wilson and FDR on) were favored by the labor union bosses (but, quite often, not by the workers themselves). All of that has dramatically changed during the last twenty years. **Now it is a coalition of big government, big business and big labor unions all against small businesses and average Americans.**

In the 2008 election, candidate Obama railed against "big business." He said, "The reason that we're not getting things done is not because we don't have good plans or good policy prescriptions. The reason is because it's not our agenda that's being moved forward in Washington – it's the agenda of the oil companies, the insurance companies, the drug companies and the special interests who dominate on a day-to-day basis in terms of legislative activity."[1] But as pointed out clearly by Timothy Carney in his book, *Obamanomics,* "This anti-corporate rhetoric is precisely the opposite of the reality. In truth, President Obama's policy prescriptions spell profits for the biggest and most well-connected businesses." Carney went on to point out, "Obama's healthcare reform, stimulus spending, global warming legislation and auto industry bailouts are ambitious packages of regulation, taxes, mandates and spending that benefit BIG business. What big corporation wouldn't welcome more taxpayer funded subsidies, regulation that crowds out competition and government mandates that drive more business to them?" It is the small companies and the taxpayers who are destroyed in this atmosphere.

This process is insidious and difficult to follow. A good example that should make it easier to comprehend this convoluted concept is to briefly review a bill recently signed by Obama entitled, "Family Smoking Prevention and Tobacco Control Act." This would seem to be a giant loss for tobacco companies. If that is so, why did the largest tobacco company (Phillip Morris) push hard for its passage from the beginning? As explained in detail in Carney's book, the big companies can afford the regulations and the little ones can't. As Professor Michael Siegel of the School of Public Health at Boston University said in *Slate,* "It is a dream come true for Philip Morris… First they make it look like they are a reformed company which really cares about reducing the toll of cigarettes and second, they protect their domination of the market and make it impossible for potentially competitive products from entering the market." Carney summarized this by writing, "This is a typical effect of Obamanomics: the President pitches Big Government as a way to curb the excesses of Big Business, but the regulations actually prop-up those Big Businesses at the expense of the smaller guys." Of course, all of these "Big" entities reciprocate with campaign donations.

Research done by the Kauffman foundation – which is dedicated to the cause of entrepreneurship in America — shows 80% of jobs (in good times and bad), are created by firms started in the last five years.² So the way to recover from the high unemployment is to help small firms with tax cuts and fewer regulations. The Obama administration is doing the opposite and his efforts are being funded by George Soros, the self-serving, economydestroying billionaire.

This is a sad commentary. With all of the ethics and values teaching squeezed out of our schools, the manipulators have free rein to "wheel and deal." Of course the Communists watch and enjoy as they see capitalism killing itself through government policies.

References
Obamanomics, Timothy Carney, 2009.

Chapter Twenty One Notes
1. Chicago Tribune, July 31, 2007.
2. Kauffman,org.

CHAPTER TWENTY-TWO

> **Goal No. 38:** Transfer some of the powers of arrest from the police to social agencies. Treat all behavioral problems as psychiatric disorders which no one but psychiatrists can understand or treat.
> **Goal No. 39:** Dominate the psychiatric profession and use mental health laws as a means of gaining coercive control over those who oppose Communist goals.

When I first heard President Obama talk about having some **special type of police force** that would report directly to him, Goal No. 38 came immediately to mind. I couldn't believe what I had heard. As with many of these Goals, they seemed far-fetched and impossible in 1958. But during his Presidential campaign on July 2, 2008, Obama said, "We cannot continue to rely on our military in order to achieve the national security objectives we've set. We've got to have a civilian national security force that's just as powerful, just as strong, just as well-funded." Apparently the negative public reaction to that statement caused him not to mention it again, but it shows how the progressives think, and it left this author with a chilling feeling. Think about Obama's statement. Why does he feel the need for a "special type" of police force reporting directly to him? What is wrong with the local police, the county sheriffs and the state police who are already in place? We don't need a Gestapo-type network reporting directly to the President. It's a frightening prospect!

Other areas of these two Goals are more subtle and difficult for a layman to analyze. A study of history shows that the Communists definitely use psychology extensively after they have taken over a country to condition the people for the changes to come. It was many years ago when the first head of the World Federation of Mental Health, Dr. Brock Chisholm, made it very clear how he and others in the field would help prepare us for the cultural breakdown that Gamsci stated would be required to set the stage for America to fall. Dr Brock said, "The pretense is made that to do away with right and wrong would produce uncivilized people, immorality, lawlessness and social chaos. The fact is that most psychiatrists and psychologists and other respected people have escaped from moral chains and are able to think freely."[1] Is this a dream or are all of these improbable things actually happening?

So as the mental health people with these views continue to condition us through our schools, the media and elsewhere, they also have an "Ace in the Hole" when needed for a quick fix. Anyone who openly stands in their way can be branded as insane and dealt with accordingly. The progressives have used this for years. Attempts were made in this way against Whittaker Chambers after he testified that Alger Hiss was a Communist traitor. A psychiatrist who had never examined Chambers testified *under oath* that Chambers was a psychopath. If Chambers had not had strong supporters in Congress, he could have well been "hauled away." Also, even first lady Eleanor Roosevelt got into the act. In her column *My Day* for August 4, 1948 she branded the testimony of Elizabeth Bentley in exposing high government officials as Communists as, "the fantasy story of this evidently neurotic lady." Still later, a man from California was committed to a mental institution, simply because of public utterances against the United Unions. Unfortunately he was not well enough "connected" to be spared.[1]

The bottom line is that, in the not too distant future, these rare examples could become commonplace, as mental health laws are used to silence and put away detractors or anyone questioning government policies.

References
Walking Targets, B. K. Eakman, Midnight Whistter Publishing, 2007.
Brainwashing, Edward Hunter, Pyramid Books, 1958.

Chapter Twenty Two Note
1. *None Dare Call it Treason – 25 Years Later*, John Stormer, Liberty Bell Press, 1992.

CHAPTER TWENTY-THREE

Goal No. 40: Discredit the family as an institution. Encourage promiscuity and easy divorce.
Goal No. 41: Emphasize the need to raise children away from the negative influence of parents. Attribute prejudices, mental blocks, and retarding of children to the suppressive influence of parents.

Goal No. 40 is one Goal that needs little comment, as almost everyone knows something of the facts in this area. From 1958 to 1990, the divorce rate increased over 100%, to where one out of every two marriages ended in divorce. It has flattened out for the last 20 years, but for an even more troubling reason: there are fewer now marrying, since a huge number of people simply cohabitate. Of those who eventually do marry, incredibly, over half of them cohabited prior to marriage.[1] **In 1958, the cohabitation rate was almost zero!**

The culmination of this staggering trend was summarized in an article in the St. Petersburg Times (August 17, 2011) when it reported that the number of Americans with children who live together without marrying has increased twelvefold since 1970. The report says **children now are more likely to have unmarried parents than divorced parents!**

The Phyllis Schlafly Report of January 2011 also reported some of the results of this sad trend: "Forty-five years ago, a liberal in Lyndon Johnson's Labor Department, Daniel Patrick Moynihan, shocked the nation with a report called 'The Negro Family: The Case for National Action.' The Great Society's welfare handouts to women were breaking up black families by making husbands irrelevant. Since the Moynihan Report, out-of-wedlock births in the United States have grown to 72.3% for blacks, 52.5% for Hispanics and 28.6% for whites. For the population as a whole, out-of-wedlock births have risen from 6% in 1960 to 40.6% today." [The "Great Society" Section of Chapter 18 also discusses this important, but tragic situation].

As with all of these Goals, people can explain away the results, citing other causes and other reasons, insisting that none of them have anything to do with communism. That is possible, but it is very significant that all of these were documented as specific Goals of worldwide communism fifty years ago and they continue to be accomplished – each and every one!

As for Goal No. 41, it is a long established goal of the progressives to get the children out of the home and into government schools at the earliest possible age. As tax policies and inflation have purposely been created to force women into the workforce, the daycare industry has boomed. Having government daycare or "Head Start" type programs is the logical consequence of these economic policies. Generations are now growing up with very bitter children who believe they have been abandoned and are not loved. After school some go home to an empty house with unsupervised Cable TV and the Internet. Worse, some don't go home at all, but rather to gang activities where they get the "belonging" they never receive from their absent parents. Still worse but commonplace, many only have a single parent. Any wonder why so many of today's young people are hostile and bitter and strike out at society? [Ann Coulter's book, *Godless,* has an important Chapter of this topic].

Chapter 18 (Goal No. 32) briefly discusses the disastrous law passed in 1965 as part of the Great Society legislation. The socalled, "Aid to Families with Dependent Children" (AFDC) bill was the key ingredient that put in motion the destruction of black families in America. Paying young women more and more money for each and every illegitimate child she bore as long as no male (father or not) was in the house, was obviously a recipe for failure. While these policies also affected white women, the proportion of blacks was, as planned, overwhelming. The sad stories from this blunder are numerous. An interesting article in the Washington Post told about a recent example of this in a high school in Alexandria, Virginia. The teacher was frustrated about how poorly some of the students were performing. The class included both African-Americans and black kids who had recently emigrated from Africa. In a moment of exasperation, the teacher blurted out this question to the native born students: "Why don't you American guys study like the kids from Africa?" An American black replied, "It's because they have fathers who kick their butts and make them study." The teacher then asked the American blacks to raise their hands if they had a father in the home. Not one hand went up. This showed (with an admittedly small sample) that it isn't a matter of race and it isn't about money, as this school had so much money that every student had been given a laptop computer. The basic lack of a father in the home was the key defining difference. The 1996 Welfare Reform addressed this issue when the Republican Congress pressed President Bill Clinton into signing the bill. Unfortunately, before the tremendous long term benefits could take hold, President Obama had those desperately needed reforms repealed as a part of the hidden items in the Stimulus Bill shoved through Congress with little time allowed for anyone to even read the bill.[2]

SIDE NOTE: From Marxism to Feminism: The planned destruction of the American family Statement of Bill Wood FC-8 Hearing on Waste, Fraud, and Abuse July 17, 2003 TESTIMONY FOR THE UNITED STATES WAYS AND MEANS COMMITTEE

The planned destruction of the family was part of the Communist agenda from its inception by Karl Marx and Frederic Engels. It became government policy in the USSR in about 1917. It was so successful in the USSR that it threatened to destroy society in the USSR. Curiously, while in the 1940s the USSR took steps to repair the damages its family-hostile policies had caused, American Communists imported the Soviet agenda for the planned destruction of the family into the USA. It has been and continues to be promoted by left-leaning liberals in the West ever since.

Reference
Understanding the Times, David A. Noebel, Summit Press, 2006.

Web References: family.org (Focus on the Family). afa.net (American Family Association).

Chapter Twenty Three Notes
1. familylifeculturewatch.com.
2. The Phyllis Schlafly Report, March 2010.

CHAPTER TWENTY-FOUR

Goal No. 42: Create the impression that violence and insurrection are legitimate aspects of the American tradition; that students and special-interest groups should rise up and use "united force" to solve economic, political or social problems.*

During the 1960's and 70's, riots became a way of life for the first time in United States history. There had been other outbreaks in the past, but the 60's brought on never-ending violence. The leftists used the Vietnam War as their excuse. The following paragraphs are excerpts taken from the Book, *The Manchurian President*, by Aaron Klein:

> The Students for a Democratic Society (SDS) had been established in late 1959 as an extremist student activist organization that went on to spearhead the 1960's anti-Vietnam War movement. A *Discover the Networks* profile notes that SDS aspired to overthrow U.S. democratic institutions, remake the American government in a Marxist image, and help our enemies be victorious on the battlefield in Vietnam. Many key SDS members were "red-diaper babies," children of parents who were Communist activists in the 1930's.

---

*Sounds exactly like the "Occupy Wall Street" movement of today!

It was at the Democrat Convention in Chicago that the SDS would make its play for national power, as SDS protestors fomented a riot with the intention of sinking the nomination of pro-war liberal candidate Hubert Humphrey. One of the SDS splinter groups, the Weathermen, led in part by Bill Ayers [later to be colleague of Barack Obama], sought the downfall of the U.S. government ... The new Weathermen entity dissolved SDS and formed a terrorist collective in its place, which was given the name Weather Underground. The Weather Underground would go on to bomb the New York City police headquarters in 1970, the United States Capital in 1971 and the Pentagon in 1972. The group was responsible for some 30 bombings...
Ayers founded the Weathermen with his wife Bernardine Dohrn, who was also one of the main leaders of the domestic terrorist group. Ayers summed up the organizations ideology: Kill all the rich people. Break up their cars and apartments. Bring the revolution home. Kill your parents.

The revolution groups up until that time and even later were following the Marxists model; i.e., violent overthrow. It was only later that the radicals began to realize what Gramsci had said forty years earlier. Finally, Saul Alinsky wrote the book that changed everything. The book was the training manual for Barack Obama. Alinsky's, *Rules for Radicals* outlined a practical method to actually accomplish, in a Western culture such as America, what had to be done, and more importantly, how to do it right. In a **Letter to the Editor** to *The Boston Globe* published on August 31, 2008, Alinsky's son David gushed about how well Obama had learned his father's teachings, as displayed at the Democratic National Convention:

> ALL the elements were present: the individual stories told by real people of their situations and hardships, the packed-to-the rafters crowd, the crowd's chanting of key phrases and names, the action on the spot of texting andphoning to show instant support and commitment to jump into the political battle, the rallying selections of music, the setting of the agenda by the power people. **The**

Democratic National Convention had all the elements of the perfectly organized event, Saul Alinsky style.

Barack Obama's training in Chicago by the great community organizers is showing its effectiveness. It is an amazingly powerful format, and the method of my late father always works to get the message out and get the supporters on board. **When executed meticulously and thoughtfully, it is a powerful strategy for initiating change and making it really happen. Obama learned his lesson well.**

I am proud to see that my father's model for organizing is being applied successfully beyond local community organizing to affect the Democratic campaign in 2008. It is a fine tribute to Saul Alinsky as we approach his 100th birthday.

L. David Alinksy

(Emphasis added)

In 2009, former Communist David Horowitz published a pamphlet analyzing the influence Alinsky's ideas had over Obama. In the pamphlet entitled *Barack Obama's Rules for Revolution: The Alinsky Model*, Horowitz writes:

> [*The*] *failure of many of our younger activists to understand the art of communication has been disastrous, writes Alinsky.* What he really means is their **honesty is disastrous**, their failure to understand the art of miss-communication. This is the precise art that he teaches radicals who are trying to impose socialism on a country whose people understand that socialism destroys freedom. **Don't sell it as socialism, sell it as "progressivism," "economic democracy" or "social justice."** (Emphasis added)

Horowitz continues, explaining the strategy of working within the system until you can accumulate enough power to destroy it. That was what sixties radicals called "boring from within." It was a strategy that the New Left despised, even as Alinsky and his followers practiced it. Alinsky and his followers infiltrated the *War on Poverty*, made alliances with the Democrat Party and secured funds from the federal government. Like termites, they set about to eat away at the foundations of the building in expectation that one day they could cause it to collapse. Alinsky's advice can be summed up in the following way: *Even though you are at war with the system, don't confront it as an opposing army; join it and undermine it as a fifth column from within.*

They were all setting the stage, waiting for the time when they could make their move. That time was finally here as Barack Obama proudly exclaimed at the height of his presidential campaign: **"We are the ones we've been waiting for!"**[1]

References
You Can Still Trust the Communist, Fred Schwarz and David Noebel, 2010.
The Manchurian President, Aaron Klein.
Rules for Radicals, Saul Alinsky.
*Barrack Obama's Rules for Revolution: The Alinsky Mode*l, David Horowitz.

Chapter Twenty Four Note
1. humanevents.com/article.php?id=27976.

CHAPTER TWENTY-FIVE

Goal No. 43: Overthrow all dictatorships before native populations are ready for self-government.

After World War II, most everyone was ready for a fresh start and a new way to prevent further wars and to reduce tensions and future conflicts. No doubt pushed on by the Communists behind the scenes (as we now know), the so-called "colonial powers" were shamed into removing control over all of their former domains outside of their own boundaries. Many of these Colonies were not at all prepared for self-government, but were quickly abandoned to fend for themselves, as the Western countries were anxious to shed these responsibilities and to stop the outcries from their critics. Numerous countries, particularly in Africa, were abandoned. Of course the Communists took maximum advantage of these situations. As always, they were not interested in helping the people. They were only interested in taking advantage of situations for their own selfish and evil goals. Several specific countries affected by this turn of events are covered in Chapter One. There are many other sad examples.

CHAPTER TWENTY-SIX

Goal No. 44: Internationalize the Panama Canal.

As with several of these Goals, the Communists underestimated how far the gullible and uninformed American people could be pushed. With the major media so biased and with most people just minding their own business, trying to make a living and raise their families, significant events take place without much notice. The Communists' goal was to get the U.S. out of Panama and relinquish control of the Canal. Instead, they were able to accomplish far more. A treaty was signed by Panama and the United States in 1903 that allowed the U.S. to build the Canal and to control it in "perpetuity." Other countries had tried to build a canal and had lost thousands of lives. Because of the dangers, technologies required and costs involved, no other country had a chance to succeed. Panama recognized this and realized the bonanza it would be to their country economically if a Canal were constructed. They also realized that no country would do all of this without keeping control. So a fair treaty was signed and all went well – until September 1, 1977. On that date the Democrat controlled Senate, relentlessly pushed by President Carter, passed by a **one vote margin** a Bill to abrogate the long standing treaty. Not only did we give up control, but a company from Communist China moved in to take over operations. Did Skousen have insight or not?

Reference
Death Knell of the Panama Canal, G. Russell Evans, 1999.

CHAPTER TWENTY-SEVEN

Goal No. 45: Repeal the Connally Reservation so the United States cannot prevent the World Court from seizing jurisdiction over domestic problems. Give the World Court Jurisdiction over nations and individuals alike.

Only two years after the Skousen book was written, the first shots were fired. The battle was described in TIME magazine of September 5, 1960:

> Throughout Washington this week began the opening shots of a battle over whether or not the U.S. will work wholeheartedly to help develop a world rule of law. The battleground was the 83rd annual meeting of the American Bar Association. Drawn up on one side were the forces that want the U.S. to lead in establishing a workable system of international law, on the other a determined rear guard, that is ready to fight tooth-and-nail to halt a necessary practical step. Point at issue is the so-called Connally Reservation, by which the U.S. reserves the right to label any international dispute involving itself as a "domestic" issue and thus escape jurisdiction by the World Court at The Hague.

Notice how TIME magazine states the "facts" in such a biased way, even back in 1960. Those fighting to preserve our heritage are referred to as the "rear guard." They then refer to this group as fighting to halt a, "necessary practical step." This was not an

145

editorial, but supposedly a factual news report. With this type of reporting on almost all fronts for over 50 years, the real miracle is that there are any clear thinkers left in America! Of course there probably wouldn't be except that in recent years, talk radio, the Internet, FOX NEWS and the Tea Party have come to the rescue. For those wanting a concise summary of the day's important news, check out: TheBlaze.com.

In the fifty years since this TIME article appeared, a subtle approach has been used to essentially accomplish this Goal. Check out "Google" and find that all of the open debates and references to this important legislation ended over thirty years ago. The law wasn't changed, just increasingly ignored.

CONCLUSIONS

We are now living through a very dangerous period. Most would concede that the two gravest external and internal threats we have as a nation at this moment in history are the Communists and the radical Muslins. Both have openly stated over and over again that they wish to control the world. President Obama was raised in a Muslim culture, went to Muslim schools and had parents who were Marxist and Muslims. Almost every friend and mentor he has had in his entire life has a Muslin or Marxist background. He had never even been in mainland America until he was an adult. He was completely unfamiliar with our heritage and our culture. As Sean Hannity readily summarized in his recent book, "We're all known by the company we keep, and Barack Obama consistently – and deliberately – keeps company with hard leftists… He couldn't be more of a Manchurian candidate if he were auditioning for the role in the movies. **This stuff is just too bizarre for most Americans to process: an actual Marxist in the White House."**[1] One needs to put this in context to really absorb it. As Hannity says, it is too bizarre to mentally process. Think of WWII where we were fighting Japan and Germany. What if our President during that war had been raised and schooled in Japan and his parents had been lifelong Nazis, along with most of his teachers, friends and advisors? How concerned would we have been? Sadly, that is not a farfetched analogy.

Many times people previously unfamiliar with the material presented in this book jump to the conclusion: "Everyone in the government must be a Communist." That, of course, is not true. Only a very small percentage in any country taken over by the Reds have been Communists. They have always used the dogooders, the dupes and the "useful idiots" (Stalin's term) to do their bidding. So, how is it possible to explain all of the happenings of the past fifty years as outlined in this book? Actually it is fairly easy to explain. As stated several times already, most people are just minding their own business, going to work, taking care of the kids, going to school, going to church, volunteering at the PTA, etc. They are not driven by some external goal and they assume that everyone else is doing the same thing. Americans have also accepted the ridiculous adage that it is not polite to discuss "politics and religion." What two topics could possibly be more important to discuss? Unfortunately, those dedicated to the cause of turning America into a Socialist state are "driven" to accomplish their goal. Why they are willing to sacrifice so much to destroy their own country is harder to explain.

The fact is that a few dedicated individuals can control a large group because they are united by a common goal and are willing to work hard to accomplish it. For an overly simplified example, imagine a Club with 100 members. The Chairman is trying to get someone to volunteer to take on the job of "lining-up" all of the monthly guest speakers for the next year. Making all of those calls and arrangements is a very time consuming task. However, Joe quickly raises his hand to do it. Everyone is very appreciative of Joe for making this sacrifice. As the year goes by, very few realize that while every speaker is speaking on various important issues, they are all from the leftist point of view. Bottom line is that 99 people are getting influenced (brainwashed) by the efforts of just one person in their group. Worst yet, the motivated culprit is highly thought of because he is willing to do all of the extra work. Magnify that a thousand times over in every walk of life and you can see the potential.

It is also important to understand how the decades of the 30's and 40's fit so disastrously into the destruction of America. During the deep depression of the 1930's, recruiting intellectuals and others into Marxism was a much easier task than at other times.

At that time it looked as though capitalism was a failure. (Some of the Reference Books already listed show that the depression was actually caused by incorrect government intervention, not by capitalism). Nevertheless, the economic conditions were ripe for massive recruitment. No sooner had all of these additional citizens been recruited into communism, then in the 1940's the Soviet Union became our ally in the fight against Nazi Germany. Therefore, if the State Department or any other department of government or any university hired an open Communist to fill a position, what is the problem? They were all "on our side" in this Great War! Unfortunately, after WWII when the U.S.S.R. turned on us very quickly and the Cold War began, all of the Communists were still in place throughout all of our institutions. Since records of who belonged to which political party were obviously not kept, the "good guys" had no way of knowing who the "bad guys" were. When their "words and actions" began to identify them, a few people in authority started noticing and became quite concerned. John Kennedy and Joe McCarthy were two in public office who expressed this concern. Later, Senator McCarthy led the charge to actually do something about it. Of course, that led to his destruction. In an overly simplified nutshell, that was how the wrong people got into the right position to facilitate the progress towards the 45 Goals documented here. It doesn't get any better in recent times, as we have seen.

During his election campaign, President Obama repeatedly talked about "fundamentally changing America." Many people took that in a good way, which is one reason he was elected. For me it was a little eerie. It brought back to my mind an incident that my father had told me about when I was only a teenager and at that time I did not realize its significance. I have never heard or read anything about this anywhere since. My dad had been an Army Officer during WWI. At the time this incident occurred in the mid 1930's he was a civilian, managing the airport at South Bend, Indiana. Thirty years later in the 1960's, my dad told me about the time he was unexpectedly visited by the Army Chief of Staff. In apparently a very private, hush – hush meeting at his airport, he was told that the top military brass had gotten together and decided that if President Roosevelt used the catastrophic depression presently going on in our country as an excuse to declare martial law in order to establish a dictatorship, the top military people had agreed among themselves that they were going to ignore Roosevelt's orders and come out on "the side of the people." I never asked for details. I didn't know or understand enough to ask. I don't know if the General came to him because my dad was the manager of an airport or because he had been an Army officer, still in the Reserves. I also didn't ask if he knew how many others were informed. My dad was never a "political" person. This conversation just came up one time and was never discussed again. It was only much later, after I had read various books that discussed how many of Roosevelt's leftist confidents had urged him to "make the move" that I then realized the significance of what my father had said and how close we had come. That same fear was later revisited when I heard Obama's Chief of Staff talk about never "letting a crisis go to waste."[2] Déjà vu!

Many people now feel like the situation is hopeless. While our country has been destroyed in many ways, the good news is that our country has come closer to a "takeover" in the past than most people realize. Each time, through the grace of God, the disaster was averted. I believe it is informative and even encouraging to review those perilous times when we were on the edge. Many people reading the following summaries will have lived through these events, but had no idea at the time at how close to the cliff we were as a country – yet each time we were spared.

The first "close call" is the one mentioned above. What would have happened if FDR had followed the advice of his Progressive advisors and made the move towards martial law and dictatorship? Would the military's counter have been effective, or would the people have supported Roosevelt? Would chaos have resulted? Close call!

The second "close call" came in 1944. In that election year FDR was running for a fourth term (I guess he decided it was better to stay on indefinitely as the elected President and "transform" our country that way, rather than the approach feared by the military). At any rate, he decided to drop Vice President

Henry Wallace from the ticket. It is very rare for a President to do that. Some say that Americans were becoming increasingly skeptical of him and he needed a mid-westerner on the ticket to give it a better balance. Whatever the reason, Wallace unexpectedly got the boot and Harry Truman was FDR's new V-P running mate. What's the point? If Wallace had stayed on, he would have become our president instead of Truman when FDR died. Not familiar with Wallace? Four years later, in 1948 he ran against Truman on the Progressive Party ticket and was officially endorsed by the Communist Party USA! A lifelong radical Socialist with numerous Communist connections would have become our president, if he had not been replaced as V-P by FDR. Some would say that sounds like what we have with Obama. But the difference is probably worse. At that time the USSR was in full swing to back Wallace at every turn. Also, there were no FOXTV, talk radio, Tea Party and the Internet. The citizens would have likely never known what hit them until it was too late. Our country was spared a horrendous ending by what seemed at the time to be a minor political decision. David Horowitz summed up this scenario when he wrote:

> My parents, who were card-carrying Communists, never referred to themselves as Communists but always as "progressives," as did their friends and political comrades. The Progressive Party was created by the Communist Party to challenge Harry Truman in the 1948 election, because he opposed the spread of Stalin's empire. The Progressive Party was led by Henry Wallace and was the vehicle chosen by the Communists to lead their followers out of the Democratic Party …

The third "close call" came in 1963 when President Kennedy was assassinated. This one is going to take a little background to understand and chances are you would not have heard this explanation before. In 1963, I was the Director of the Greater St. Louis *Goldwater for President Organization*. Unknown to most people, Senator Goldwater was gaining traction against Kennedy (we were taking polls and the media was hiding this startling turn of events). Goldwater's book, *The Conscience of a Conservative,* had become a national best seller. In addition, JFK was a close friend of Goldwater and they had agreed that if Goldwater became the Republican nominee, they would travel the country together and hold "Lincoln — Douglas" type debates. Informed conservatives believe this would have catapulted Goldwater to victory, not because Kennedy was a weak debater, but because in that time period, most people had never heard anyone articulate the true conservative point of view. When they heard it, a vast majority of Americans responded with "that's the way I believe, but have never heard anyone state it." Much like when Rush Limbaugh first burst on the talk radio scene. Almost every early caller expressed that they had never heard anyone before who, "believed like they did."

At the time the USSR was on a roll and would do anything to prevent the knowledgeable anti-Communist Goldwater from becoming an American president. While Kennedy was far more anti-Communist than any modern day Democrat, his State Department was filled with leftists. As detailed in Chapter One, the Soviets had for years counted on our State Department to aid and abet their every move. Being aware of Goldwater's writings and stands in the Senate, the Soviets were terrified at the possibility of his election. They no doubt feared that Goldwater would come in and "clean out" the State Department that had been their "friend" for decades (Eisenhower had been far too easy going to really shake up the system. In fact he resisted Senator McCarthy's efforts). With this in mind, at a meeting of our St. Louis Goldwater group, the question came up wondering if the Soviets would try to assassinate Goldwater. We concluded that if they made Goldwater a martyr and if they were found to be involved, it would insure the election of a hard-nose, Republican anti-Communist and shut up the leftist press and State Department for years. Later that evening after I returned home, I thought about it and I realized that if Reds wanted to make such a risky and drastic move, it would be Kennedy they would assassinate, not Goldwater. This would assure a landslide victory for the Democrats (sympathy for JFK) and no interruption in their world wide goals. I actually wrote this horrid scenario in a memo that I sent out to the Board members later that week.

Why do I feel that this assassination was a "close call?" That again requires some background, not familiar to most Americans. The stage had been set for the government to use this type of crises to take control and to pick up or shut up all of the outspoken conservatives. Farfetched? Hardly! Look what the government did to the American-born Japanese after Pearl Harbor and what Woodrow Wilson had done during WWI to those speaking out against his policies. They were jailed! In the early 60's, much like in today's Tea Party movement, people were waking up and they were upset. Anti-communism study groups were forming all over the country. Experts such as Dr. Fred Schwarz, Cleon Skousen, Herb Philbrick, Robert Morris and others were speaking to huge crowds and holding week-long seminars. Excellent new books were being widely purchased [*None Dare Call It Treason*, a self published book, sold more than seven million copies. Phyllis Schlafly's, *A Choice not an Echo*, sold millions. Dr. Fred Schwarz's, *You Can Trust the Communist* was a best seller]. People were becoming informed. When conservatives become active, that is when the leftists become alarmed. **They understand that an informed people are the only danger to their long term Socialist dreams**. Concerned conservatives were being labeled as hate mongers (sound familiar?).

With that as background, it was only natural that when President Kennedy was assassinated in Dallas (a hot bed of conservative rallies), the media instantly labeled the rightwing as being responsible for his death. That line took hold because of all of the slander the media poured out in the days prior. The average citizen who had not been actively involved politically (a large majority) accepted that conservatives were responsible. Remember, there was no talk radio, Fox News, Tea Party or the Internet to counter any of these charges. I personally had to leave work early that day. People whom I had known for years were suddenly circling my office with hate in their eyes, as I was known to be a leader in the conservative movement in St. Louis. Ironically, many of those with threatening looks were not only friends, but had readily accepted Goldwater brochures from me from time to time. No more! In their minds, they had been preconditioned by the media to believe that people like me had murdered the President. I had a neighbor lady who was an active conservative. She got a call from her lifelong friend who screamed to her on the phone through tears that she was responsible for killing Kennedy! While I was known locally by the political crowd as a "Goldwater for President" spokesman, the average person would never have heard of me. Yet even someone as far down the list as I was, had my mail intercepted and held for four days. Apparently, all vocal conservatives throughout the country were on a "watch list." Incredibly, even the Chief Justice of the U.S. Supreme Court Earl Warren went on national radio to blame "the climate of hate" as the cause of the President's murder. He said this without any evidence.[3]

When the Japanese had been rounded up to be put in camps after Pearl Harbor, there was little outcry. Often people act and make decisions based upon emotions. It is obvious that at the time of the JFK murder, all of the outspoken conservatives could have been "picked up" without a whimper of protest. When a country loses all of the opposition voices, it is a very quick slide into a leftwing totalitarian state.

In my mind, God again intervened. A police officer "accidently" ran into Lee Harvey Oswald. Oswald panicked and shot him, assuming the officer knew what he had done. Soon thereafter, he was apprehended. Then the news that all progressives dreaded to hear came out: Not only was Oswald NOT a conservative activist, he had spent time in Russia and was a Communist sympathizer. He had married a Russian girl. It came out that he had earlier tried to murder Major General Edwin Walker. Gen. Walker was a well known and articulate anti-Communist. So the media had to face the horrifying truth that the President, philosophically speaking, had been murdered by one of their own. In my opinion, had Oswald not been caught, all of the leading "hate mongers" would have been rounded up. If not put in prison, effectively silenced for life. Surprisingly, years later President Nixon summed it up when he said (in a recently released recorded interview) that at first the media had tried to, "**… pin the assassination of Kennedy on the right wing and the Birchers.*** **(Yet) it was done by a Communist and it was the greatest hoax that has ever been perpetuated.**"

My main point is that if Oswald had not been apprehended, I am positive that the stage had been set for the conservative leaders to be silenced. A very important related issue always comes up when I relate this story to informed people. They acknowledge, as even President Nixon did, that Oswald was a Communist (or a sympathizer at the least). But a key question is, did the Soviets really train Oswald while he was in Russia to do this, or was he just a leftist nut that got "carried away?" Since nothing could have advanced their goals more than assuring that Goldwater was defeated, it was certainly feasible.

While I had predicted this possibility, for nearly twenty years I felt that it was highly unlikely that the Russian KGB (the Soviet secret police) had actually trained Oswald for this mission. I just felt they would never have taken a chance to plan such an outlandish act against such a prominent figure as the President of the United States. While it all "fit," it just seemed too farfetched. That was until May of 1981. On the 18th of May, Pope John Paul II was shot four times in an assassination attempt. The Pope, who was from Poland, had been outspoken in his support of the solidarity labor movement in Poland that was trying to gain some freedom for the Polish workers who were under total Soviet control. Later the world was stunned to find out that the assassin had been trained by the Russian KGB. I then realized that they were, in fact, capable and willing to go even that far! Planning an assassination of a President of a country is definitely feasible, if they are prepared to murder even the Pope. Incredible! The Soviets apparently realized that our media would always cover for them, even if they killed our President. That fact alone is very frightening and should be a wakeup call to all.

---

*The term "Birchers" that President Nixon used in his statement refers to a staunch Anti-Communist group known as the John Birch Society. The group was very active in the 1960's (and is still around fighting the good fight today).

The fourth "close call" came in 1979. This was Jimmy Carter's last year in office. He had successfully gutted our military, which had been going on for years. We were at that time a second rate military power, at least compared to the USSR. The Soviets had a massive ballistic missile lead over us. Also, they had an operational anti-missile system surrounding Moscow, their major population center. Incredibly, we had negotiated a treaty that allowed them to have such a defensive system, but did not allow us to have any! They also had an extensive civil defense program in place to protect many of their citizens from any offensive missiles that survived their ABM system. We had none. Peace at any price was the call of the day from the progressives. Had the Soviet leader called President Carter on the *hotline* and told him to surrender, or it would cost Americans millions of lives, there is no doubt in my mind that Carter would have capitulated. To be honest, at that hopeless point, it would have probably been the right decision. "Give me liberty or give me death" speeches don't resonate well when one is talking about 100 million casualties! So why didn't the Soviets make that call? Their whole mission was to dominate the world. Strange? Only God knows. After a few years of the Reagan military build-up in the 1980's, thankfully they had lost their opportunity.

So, do we just sit around with business as usual, expecting that God will continue to protect us? He certainly seems to have done so many times in the past, from George Washington's miraculous victory to, among other occasions, the four "close calls" listed above. Mrs. Billy Graham was quoted as saying that "if God doesn't eventually judge America, He will owe an apology to Sodom and Gomorrah." Unfortunately, I think that makes sense. I don't think we can sit idly by anymore. It is time for Christians and other concerned citizens to start making a difference. **We obviously need more prayer, but now we also need more action by informed people!**

Become informed: Read some of the books recommended here. Read a weekly conservative newsletter such as *Human Events* (there are many others). Subscribe to the monthly *Schwarz Report*. Watch FOX NEWS. Watch GBTV.com. Listen to conservative talk shows as time permits. Have your young people attend *The Summit* (summit.org). **You must be informed — not an expert, just informed.** Understand that the main purpose of most so-called mainstream news outlets is either to brainwash you or to keep you uniformed.

Take a Stand: Write Letters to the Editors. Call in a local radio talk show. Speak up at meetings and gatherings. Write your elected officials. Foreward to your friends informative emails.

Get involved: Be a leader in your Church. Become active in a political party or other political action group. Find a local Tea Party group. Most of these are made up of very informed and dedicated people. Email your friends with important information and happenings. Give of your time and donations.

Voting: In a way, we have only ourselves to blame. Only about 50% of the Christian community are even registered to vote. Of those, only 50% actually vote! We can blame the liberals and the Marxist, but if only one out of four Christians even bother to vote—we have no one to blame but ourselves.

Register now and get your friends registered. Then, get out and VOTE!

A person in any state can register very easily by going to: ChampionTheVote.com.

Check out the many websites noted herein. Most of them regularly give specific ideas on actions that need our attention at a particular time!

Keep this in mind as an encouragement. If only 1% of all adult Americans took 15 minutes a month to make their voices heard [letters, calls, etc.], humanly speaking, the political problems would be resolved. That is not asking much!!!

I have given enough references for you to do your own research. The stakes are high! Your freedom and those you care about are threatened. Be the Paul Revere of your time. With God and truth, you are in the majority!

Conclusions Notes

1. *Conservative Victory*, Sean Hannity, Harper, 2010, pg. 40.
2. *WSJ*.com, January 28, 2009.
3. *nationalreview*.com, Jonah Goldberg, April 17 2009.